Opera on CD

GW00359458

Alan Blyth was born in London. He was educated at Rugby School and at Pembroke College, Oxford, where he was on the committee of the University Opera Club. After working for Encyclopaedia Britannica as a music editor, he became a freelance music critic with *The Times* and the *Financial Times*, specialising on singers and opera. He was on the music staff of the *Daily Telegraph* from 1976 to 1990, and assistant editor of *Opera* magazine from 1967 to 1984. He is now on the magazine's editorial board. He has reviewed vocal records for *Gramophone* for the past twenty-five years. He contributes regularly to Radio 3's *Record Review* and to its series 'Interpretations on Record', and to Radio 4's 'Kaleidoscope'. He has edited three volumes of *Opera on Record*, and his other publications include *The Enjoyment of Opera*, *Remembering Britten*, and *Wagner's Ring: an Introduction*. He has contributed many entries to the *New Grove Dictionary of Opera* and to the forthcoming *Grove Dictionary of Music and Musicians*. He is record consultant to the forthcoming *Penguin Dictionary of Opera*. His interests outside music include wine and gardening.

Opera on CD

THE ESSENTIAL GUIDE TO THE BEST CD RECORDINGS OF 100 OPERAS

ALAN BLYTH

KYLE CATHIE LTD

First published in Great Britain by
Kyle Cathie Ltd
3 Vincent Square
London SW1P 2LX

Copyright © 1992 by Alan Blyth

ISBN 1 85626 056 9

A CIP catalogue record for this book is available from
the British Library

All rights reserved. No reproduction, copy or transmission
of this publication may be made without written permission.
No paragraph of this publication may be reproduced, copied
or transmitted save with written permission or in accordance
with the provisions of the Copyright Act 1956 (as amended).
Any person who does any unauthorised act in relation to this
publication may be liable to criminal prosecution and civil
claims for damages.

Alan Blyth is hereby identified as author of this work
in accordance with Section 77 of the Copyright, Designs
and Patents Act 1988.

Designed by Lorraine Estelle
Typeset by DP Photosetting
Printed in Great Britain
by Biddles Ltd, Guildford, Surrey

CONTENTS

CONTENTS

INTRODUCTION

This guide is intended both for experienced opera-lovers confused by the bewildering number of discs now on the market and for newcomers keen to build a basic, varied and worthwhile collection of CDs. Where the choice of versions of a particular piece is large, I have often opted for sets that have stood the test of time and proved lasting winners in their sphere. In some cases I have drawn on reissues of pre-war or immediately post-war recordings in mono only (e.g. the De Sabata/Callas *Tosca*) that seem musically, vocally and dramatically superior to anything that has since emerged even when that means accepting dated sound. However, I have in these cases suggested alternatives of more recent vintage in modern sound. In the case of works of the eighteenth-century or earlier, I have taken into account the claims of period-instrument performance without allowing that to dominate my choice.

The advent of the CD has allowed many notable recordings of the past to be digitally re-mastered to their and our advantage. At the same time it has seen a burgeoning in the number of new versions of operas available. Of course that has increased choice, but it has often meant the spreading of talent rather thinly over a number of sets of the same work. However, fears that CD would concentrate only on the standard repertory have proved unfounded as the choice of works included here confirm, not least in the Handelian field. Yet there remains a number of operas that await a first recording.

Unfortunately insufficient care is now taken to achieve satisfactory results as regards thorough rehearsal and/or the assembling of integrated ensembles as compared with recordings made during the 1950s and '60s, the golden days of producers such as Walter Legge (EMI) and John Culshaw (Decca). Singers are often chosen because of their star status rather than because of their aptness for the role in hand.

The coming of CD has unfortunately allowed the companies to get away with accompanying material that is grossly inadequate. In the days of LP, lavish booklets for opera were almost always supplied, including full texts and translations; today the booklets are often skimpy and, in the case of reissues, sometimes omit texts altogether. With the high price being asked, in Britain at least, for CDs, this state of affairs should be put to rights. That said, the increased interest in opera owes a deal to the CD and its user-friendliness.

The listings here are presented in the chronological order of the birth-dates of the composers, which has thrown up unexpected juxtapositions. Except in the case of the most familiar repertory, I have placed each composer and work in some kind of perspective and given a resumé of the plot and/or the style of the music. This method gives the volume a historical aspect. In order to avoid too much detail I have included in the cast lists only the main characters and singers. I have avoided the symbols and/or stars that sometimes make guides of this kind impenetrable or confusing.

Inevitably any book of this kind represents a personal choice. By and large I have attempted to suppress my own likes, dislikes and prejudices, but total objectivity in matters of criticism is obviously impossible. Standards of style in singing and interpretation have changed mightily in the era of the gramophone and its modern counterparts. Fashions constantly change. Yet the great artists – Caruso, Callas, Sutherland, Domingo, to take four notable instances – remain that, however they are compared with their successors or their predecessors. They figure prominently here because they are exciting interpreters. Above all I have avoided readings that seem 'manufactured' in any way, or sound studio-bound, preferring, where possible, what is, or sounds like, a live interpretation. One thing I promise: buyers of any discs recommended here will not be bored.

I should like to thank John T. Hughes for reading manuscript and proofs, James Jolly for his help in checking as far as possible that the details here are up-to-date, and Kyle Cathie for her support and encouragement throughout.

Alan Blyth
January 1992

Claudio Monteverdi (1567–1643)

L'Orfeo. Lynne Dawson (Eurydice), Nancy Argenta (Nymph), Anne Sofie von Otter (Messenger), Diana Montague (Proserpina), Anthony Rolfe Johnson (Orfeo), Willard White (Pluto), John Tomlinson (Charon), Monteverdi Choir, English Baroque Soloists/John Eliot Gardiner. (DG Archiv 419 250–2)

Monteverdi, the first opera composer of consequence, is known to have written seven works for the stage. Of these only three survive. *L'Orfeo* was first given at Mantua in 1607. It differs from the other two in that, unusually for its time, its instrumental forces are specified. Languishing in the archives for several centuries, the piece was at last resuscitated in 1904 by the composer Vincent D'Indy. Since then it has been performed in many different editions, the more recent aiming at some kind of authenticity. Among today's conductors John Eliot Gardiner has been a leading light in the Monteverdi revival. Here he attempts to marry dramatic conviction with a stylistic unity of approach.

L'Orfeo is a deeply moving study in human passion, a setting of a text by Alessandro Striggio. Monteverdi employs expressive, extended recitative leaning over into *arioso* passages as the basis of his style. The title role falls somewhere between a tenor's and a baritone's range. It demands an understanding of Monteverdi's specific vocal style such as that provided by Anthony Rolfe Johnson in this version, which is a product of experience in the part on stage. His appeals to rescue his beloved Eurydice are passionately delivered in response to the announcement of his loved one's death by the gravely eloquent Messenger of Anne Sofie von Otter. Eurydice is purely and beautifully sung by the ethereal-voiced Lynne Dawson. A strong team of British singers versed in the idiom is to be found in support, among them Willard White's sonorous Pluto and John Tomlinson's sinister Charon. The singing of Gardiner's aptly named Monteverdi Choir is another asset.

Il ritorno d'Ulisse in Patria. Norma Lerer (Penelope), Sven Olof Eliasson (Ulysses), Kai Hansen (Telemachus), Murray Dickie (Irus), Vienna Concentus Musicus/Nikolaus Harnoncourt. (Teldec 2292-42496-2)

This is probably the greatest of Monteverdi's three surviving operas. It tells of Penelope's steadfastness and fidelity during Ulysses's long absence abroad and the importuning of her suitors followed by her happy reward when her husband at last returns to her. Monteverdi clothes the tale in music of surpassing eloquence, in particular Penelope's long monologue at the beginning of the work and in the scenes when Ulysses returns home in disguise to defeat the unwelcome suitors for his wife's hand.

Unfortunately the work has been largely neglected by the major companies, ever willing to produce another set of a Mozart opera but disregarding his great predecessor. Harnoncourt's reading is predictably arresting, his chosen scoring a fair solution to the problems set by the lack of knowledge about Monteverdi's own instrumentation. He is let down, however, by an indifferent cast. Until another, better-sung performance comes along, this one will just about suffice to indicate the score's inspiration.

L'Incoronazione di Poppea. Helen Donath (Poppea), Elisabeth Söderström (Nero), Cathy Berberian (Octavia), Paul Esswood (Otho), Giancarlo Luccardi (Seneca), Vienna Concentus Musicus/Nikolaus Harnoncourt. (Teldec 2292 42547-2)

The plot of Monteverdi's last opera, familiar from the Roman historian Tacitus, runs counter to the conventions of literary morality in allowing the adulterous love of the emperor Nero for the spoilt Poppea to triumph, leaving his wife, Octavia, distraught in exile and his friend-philosopher, Seneca, murdered for opposing his master's will. Here interpretative problems are legion. Two copies of the score, made after Monteverdi's time, survive, both containing emendations, some by other hands, including the famous love duet at the end. The voices and instrumentation used here have to be left to the discretion of the conductor. Various composers and conductors have made their editions during the Monteverdi revival this century. The most significant in recent times is the work of Harnoncourt, who has recorded the piece twice. Of his versions, the first – made in 1974 – is by far the more successful. It is a performance notable for its stimulating insights and for the special character Harnoncourt derives from his chosen, period instruments, played by virtuoso artists. He has also mastered the art, essential with this composer, of moving imperceptibly from declamation to aria. He also manages successfully the contrasts of mood so essential in this piece. In sum, the interpretation sounds as if it is living theatre, hardly surprising when Harnoncourt has conducted all the Monteverdi operas in the theatre. There is nothing here of the museum piece. Donath suggests the ruthless, teasingly seductive nature of Poppea. Nero, originally a castrato part, is sung with dedicated fervour by Söderström. Counter tenor Paul Esswood makes much of another originally castrato part, that of Poppea's deserted husband, Otho. All in all this is a creative, vivid act of reconstruction.

Recommended alternative: Richard Hickox (EMI) – this is a more fastidiously orchestrated version than Harnoncourt's but lacks its vitality. Arleen Auger is a musical, slightly too staid Poppea, Della Jones an impetuous Nero.

Henry Purcell (1659–95)

Dido and Aeneas. Lynne Dawson (Belinda), Anne Sofie von Otter (Dido), Nigel Rogers (Sorceress, Sailor), Stephen Varcoe (Aeneas) English Concert Ch, English Concert/ Trevor Pinnock. (DG Archiv 427 624-2)

This is the first true opera by a British composer written, to a play by Nahum Tate, for a London girls' school. Unlike all his other pieces for the stage, it has no spoken dialogue. Its succinct, one-act form tells the same story, in under an hour, as Berlioz's vast epic *Les Troyens* (qv). Aeneas, seeking refuge from Troy, is driven by a storm to Carthage where he falls in love with Queen Dido. After they have enjoyed one night together, he is called away, through the intervention of the Sorceress, by higher powers to go to Italy. Distraught at his precipitate departure, Dido sings her famous Lament before stabbing herself and dying on a funeral pyre.

This single-act work has been performed in many different ways – nobody quite knows for certain its original form. This one, using period instruments but strong, modern voices (not the etiolated, vibrato-less ones found on the admired Parrott set on Chandos), seems to follow sensible choices under Pinnock's diligent direction. Von Otter is a queenly, dignified, impassioned Dido, singing with surpassing beauty in the Lament. Dawson is bright and clear as Belinda, Dido's soulmate, who advises the Queen to surrender to Aeneas's advances. Varcoe is a manly, pleasing Aeneas. The set uses a tenor, rather than the usual mezzo, as the Sorceress: Rogers's performance almost justifies the choice, and he doubles as the jolly sailor. Playing and recording are exemplary.

Recommended alternatives: Anthony Lewis (Decca) – this 1961 performance, now at mid-price, remains the best of modern-instrument performances chiefly because of Janet Baker's all-consuming, intense Dido and Lewis' scholarly, authoritative conducting. Geraint Jones (EMI) – this 1952 disc, made after performances at the first Mermaid Theatre, has Kirsten Flagstad's grandly moving Dido and Thomas Hemsley's articulate Aeneas.

The Fairy Queen. Nancy Argenta, Lynne Dawson, Isabelle Desrochers, Charles Daniels, Mark le Brocq, Jean-Paul Fouchécourt, Bernard Looner, Thomas Randle, Bernard Deletré, François Bazola, Thomas Lander and others, Les Arts Florissants/William Christie. (Harmonia Mundi HMC90 1308/9)

Although not strictly an opera, this work has the force of a drama. It is loosely based on a seventeenth-century adaptation of Shakespeare's *A Midsummer Night's Dream* and offers a sequence of masque-like interludes together with dances which originally separated the dialogue. The original work was immensely long: the music alone runs more than two hours. Here it is easily contained on two CDs in a vivid recording that followed stage performances at the Aix-en-Provence Festival in 1989. As a consequence real theatrical excitement is conveyed. Christie, a pastmaster in this era of music, brings the score to exciting life, and exploits its many moods, ranging from the comedy of the Drunken Poet and the Corydon/Mopsa episodes, through the mysteries of the Night music, to the eloquence of the famous Plaint. There is nothing here of mere historical interest; everything is played and sung with immediacy and enthusiasm. The predominantly French cast of singers, all idiomatic in English, is, however, headed by two lovely British sopranos in Argenta and Dawson (particularly special in the Plaint). A much older, finely sung and played account on L'Oiseau-Lyre, conducted by Anthony Lewis, ought to be resuscitated on CD.

George Frideric Handel (1685–1759)

Handel was one of the most sought-after opera composers of his day. His earliest pieces for the opera house were written for Hamburg, his mature ones mostly for the King's Theatre and Covent Garden in London. Some forty works were staged in the latter theatres over the thirty years between 1711 and 1741, an unprecedented span. After Handel's death the majority of them lay neglected and forgotten since *opera seria*, the form in which he wrote, went out of fashion, partly because many of the leading roles were written for castrati, a voice that became unfashionable not long after Handel's demise.

In the latter half of this century his reputation as an opera composer (some of his oratorios have always retained their popularity) has undergone an extraordinary and wholly justified renaissance through the efforts of dedicated Handelians, with the castrato roles sung by mezzos or counter-tenors. At first, his operas were appreciated only by specialists, but in the past few years, not least because of the advent of period-instrument performance and of CD, they have become known and enjoyed by a more general public, which has come to realise that within the constrictions of *opera seria* Handel achieved marvels in conveying the conflicting emotions and predicaments of his characters, most of them drawn from legend or antiquity. Here human foibles – love, jealousy, envy, hatred, intrigue, tragedy – and many supernatural matters, chiefly pertaining to magic, were unerringly delineated in music of wide-ranging power. Several important pieces still await recording, but enough is now available to prove conclusively the case for Handel. They are reviewed here in order of composition. The most notable gap in the CD catalogue is the late work, *Semele*, written with the stage in mind but first presented as an oratorio. One hopes the Gardiner performance will soon re-appear.

Amadigi di Gaula. Jennifer Smith (Oriana), Eiddwen Harrhy (Melissa), Nathalie Stutzmann (Amadigi), Bernarda Fink (Dardano), Musiciens de Louvre/Marc Minkowski. (Erato 2292-45490-2)

This is one of the earliest (1715) of Handel's successes in London and one of the most economic in terms of length and number of characters. It shows Handel's immediate ability to create drama within formality. It is the second of his magic operas: set in Gaul, it describes how the scheming sorceress Melissa tries to entice Amadigi away from the lovely Oriana, who is also desired, hopelessly, by Dardano, Prince of Thrace. Although there are only four main characters, all taken by high voices (the hero is written for an alto-castrato), Handel wholly avoids monotony through his skill in giving their emotions expression in a succession of wonderfully varied numbers, each appropriate to the situation in hand.

This set is notable for the conducting of the young Minkowski, whose lithe, direct reading is always responsive to the emotional turbulence voiced by the principals. His Musiciens du Louvre play with a discipline and character that sound right and natural. His singers have been chosen with an ear to their aptness for the characters they portray. Stutzmann is a fresh, ardent Amadigi, singing Handel's divisions with complete assurance. Her true contralto timbre is keenly contrasted with the brighter mezzo of Fink, who is superb in the long, lamenting aria, 'Pena tiranna'.

Similarly Jennifer Smith's soft-grained, somewhat languid singing as Oriana is nicely contrasted with Harrhy's more incisive,
fiery manner as Melissa. Harrhy, always an accomplished Handelian, dispatches the awkward 'Vanne lunghi' with élan and finds
the pathos of the sorceress's dying moments. To complete
pleasure, the recording is exemplary in tone and balance.

Acis and Galatea. Claron McFadden (Galatea), John Mark
Ainsley (Acis), Rogers Covey-Crump (Damon), Michael
George (Polyphemus), King's Consort/Robert King. (Hyp-
erion CDA 66361/2)

This delightful work, a masque or pastoral serenade, was written
in 1717 while Handel was court composer to the Duke of
Chandos at Cannons, just outside London, where it was first
performed. It is one of his few stage works to maintain its
popularity from composition to modern times (Mozart even re-
orchestrated it; a version in German translation is available on an
Orfeo CD, conducted by Peter Schreier; another, with an
excellent cast, conducted by Trevor Pinnock, awaits issue on DG
Archiv). The story, taken from Dryden's translation of the
thirteenth book of Ovid's *Metamorphoses*, tells of the lovely sea-
nymph Galatea beloved of the shepherd Acis. Their period of
Arcadian bliss is interrupted and eventually destroyed by the
intervention of the monster Polyphemus who falls in love with
Galatea and kills the courageous Acis. On this broken idyll Handel
lavished the pure spirit of his youthful inspiration. The music for
the lovers, alone and in the joyful duet that closes Act 1, is of the
utmost beauty; that for Polyphemus presents him as a dangerous
yet oddly ridiculous character. Once Acis has been slain, Handel
writes music of elevated, tragic cut for the mourning Galatea and
chorus.

All this is carefully delineated in this 1989 recording using
period instruments. McFadden sings with artless beauty as
Galatea, Ainsley with fresh ardour as Acis, George with sonorous
bite as Polyphemus. The subsidiary character of the shepherd
Damon is mellifluously sung by Covey-Crump. The choral
singing, under King's clear direction, completes satisfaction in this
excellent issue.

Recommended alternative: John Eliot Gardiner (DG Archiv) – this earlier version is more dramatic than the above, but less accomplished in orchestral execution (in 1978 period-instrument playing was more erratic than it was to become). The performance is notable for the lovely Galatea of Norma Burrowes (whose splendid career was cruelly cut short by illness) and the vivid Acis of Anthony Rolfe Johnson.

Giulio Cesare. Valerie Masterson (Cleopatra), Janet Baker (Giulio Cesare), Della Jones (Sextus), Sarah Walker (Cornelia), James Bowman (Ptolemy), John Tomlinson (Achillas), Ch and O of the English National Opera/Charles Mackerras. (EMI CMS7 69760-2)

No doubt because it depicts a well-documented slice of history, this work was one of the first to restore Handel's reputation. Its popularity is well deserved as it shows the ardent, wilful nature of the eponymous hero and the voluptuous, minxish character of Cleopatra in a number of well-varied and marvellously apt arias, and at the same time depicts loyal Sextus, vicious, vengeful Ptolemy, and put-upon Cornelia in music wholly appropriate to *their* respective plights. It is a lengthy work given here in a reasonably full, but far from complete format, conducted by Mackerras, one of the pioneers of the Handel revival and a notable Handelian scholar.

The performance derives from a successful revival, given by the ENO in English, using modern instruments. It marked one of Janet Baker's last performances, out of very many, in the Handelian field of which she was a complete mistress. Her voice has the strength and colour to do full justice to the (originally castrato) role of Julius Caesar and she fulfils every exigent demand that the part presents. Masterson is no less adept in tone, expression and runs: she also encompasses Cleopatra's many moods with consummate ease. Bowman is suitably nasty as the preening Ptolemy, Della Jones concerned as the slighted Sextus. Sarah Walker and Tomlinson complete a strong team of 1980s Handelians, all benefiting from the experience of many performances of the opera on stage. The brand-new Harmonia Mundi set, using period instruments, is absolutely complete and also recommendable.

Tamerlano. Nancy Argenta (Asteria), Jane Findlay (Irene), Derek Lee Ragin (Tamerlano), Michael Chance (Andronico), Nigel Robson (Bajazet), René Schirrer (Leone), English Baroque Soloists/John Eliot Gardiner. (Erato 2292-45408–2)

This work was the immediate successor to *Giulio Cesare* at the King's Theatre (1724). Its plot is slender, dealing with pride, conquest, love, disguises and poisoning in the palace of the Tartar Emperor Tamburlaine after he has defeated the Turks. But it was the kind of challenge Handel revelled in, and his score for it bristles with original invention, not least in the striking power of the scenes ending Acts 2 and 3. Asteria, the Turkish princess falsely accused of betraying her father and accepting Tamburlaine as her lover, and Tamburlaine himself, who finally repents, take centre stage, but the other characters are also well catered for.

This performance, adhering closely to Handel's first thoughts and ignoring later changes, omits only three arias. Gardiner, as ever, approaches his task with a fine blend of scholarship and performing skill. All is conceived with just the urgency Handel deserves, in the event proving him a master of drama. Michael Chance, a paragon of a counter-tenor, is the most agreeable singer in an uneven cast: he takes the role of Andronico, Asteria's true love. Argenta is faultless in style as Asteria, but slightly wanting in emotional presence. Ragin is somewhat pallid in the title role, which might with advantage have been given to Chance. Ragin offers little of the exciting, bravura singing the castrato is thought to have brought to this kind of music. Robson is an assured Bajazet, one of the very few extended roles for tenor in Handel's operas. In spite of the strictures enough is achieved to make this a worthy representation of a striking work.

Alessandro. Isabelle Poulenard (Lisaura), Sophie Boulin (Rossane), René Jacobs (Alessandro), Jean Nirouët (Tassile), Stephen Varcoe (Clito), La Petite Bande/Sigiswald Kuijken. (Deutsche Harmonia Mundi GD 77109)

Written for the Haymarket Theatre in 1726, this was the first of five operas Handel composed for the rival prima donnas, Bordoni and Cuzzoni. The cast also included the noted castrato, Senesino. Handel wrote prolifically for all three throughout their respective careers. (He was a noted *Messiah* soloist much later on.) The story concerns Alexander the Great and his invasion of Macedonia. War and love alternate as the opera's themes, both treated by Handel with equal felicity. Act 1 is colourful; Act 2 deals in deeper, more emotional matters. The famed alto, Jacobs, is an authoritative, expressive Alessandro. As Lisaura and Rossane, jealous rivals for the ruler's love, Boulin and Poulenard are more limited in their execution of the fearsomely difficult music written for the original sopranos. The playing is stylish, the recording excellent.

Partenope. Kristina Laki (Partenope), Helga Müller-Molinari (Rosmira), René Jacobs (Arsace), John York Skinner (Armindo), Stephen Varcoe (Oromonte), a Petite Bande/ Sigiswald Kuijken. (Deutsche Harmonia Mundi GD 77109)

The involved plot of this comedy centres on a woman disguising herself as a man. The conventions of the characters in heroic operas of the time are cleverly guyed, and Handel responds to this conceit with many beguiling and light-hearted arias. This performance is as enjoyable as the related one of *Alessandro* with elegant period-instrument playing and an accomplished cast including Müller-Molinari as the lady who assumes male garb in pursuit of Arsace, mellifluously sung by Jacobs. As the delightful girl of the title, Laki sings with appreciable charm.

Orlando. Emma Kirkby (Dorinda), Arleen Auger (Angelica), Catherine Robbin (Medoro), James Bowman (Orlando), David Thomas (Zoroastro), Academy of Ancient Music/ Christopher Hogwood. (L'Oiseau-Lyre 430 845-2)

This is one of the greatest of Handel's operas, written in 1733 when he was at the peak of his powers as an opera (as distinct from an oratorio) composer. Based loosely on Ariosto's epic poem *Orlando furioso*, it illustrates, as well as any of the composer's work, his extraordinary ability to depict the emotional states of his characters with sympathy and understanding – and that surely is what opera is about. Orlando himself becomes mentally unhinged through unrequited love. For him Handel wrote music of high originality, authoritatively realised here by Bowman (this was one of the major roles written for the previously-mentioned Senesino). He is superb in Orlando's highly original mad scene at the end of Act 2 and in his equally inspired, hauntingly beautiful aria, with *viola d'amore obbligato*, in Act 3, excusing some rough aspiration on the singer's part elsewhere. Angelica, object of Orlando's passion, is given the benefit of Auger's lovely, but sometimes too flaccid singing. Kirkby is, as usual, bright and unsullied in tone as the charming Dorinda. But the most idiomatic Handelian singing comes from Robbin as Medoro. As the magician Zoroastro, David Thomas favours words over tone and line. Hogwood's direction lacks the inner energy and dramatic timing Handel calls for, but the recording is excellent. As a whole enough is done to suggest the work's calibre.

Alcina. Arleen Auger (Alcina), Eiddwen Harrhy (Morgana), Patrizia Kwella (Oberto), Della Jones (Ruggiero), Kathleen Kuhlmann (Bradamante), Maldwyn Davies (Oronte), John Tomlinson (Melisso), Opera Stage Ch, City of London Baroque Sinfonia/Richard Hickox. (CDS7 49771-2)

This was one of the first of Handel's operas to return to favour, largely because of the advocacy of Joan Sutherland in the title role: she undertook it, before becoming famous, in a 1957 staging in London, then repeated it under Zeffirelli in Venice, Dallas, and London in the 1960s. Her Decca recording is regrettably unavailable on CD (although an earlier, off-the-air version with her, from Cologne Radio, dating from 1959 has appeared on the Rodolphe label). The work is another piece dealing with a sorceress (Alcina) and her suborning of the knight Ruggiero's love. His beloved Bradamante disguises herself as a man to rescue Ruggiero from Alcina's clutches. Handel clothed the improbable story in music of power and well-varied expression.

This recording derives from a staging in London at the Spitalfields Festival in the late '80s. It features Auger as an accomplished Alcina, but by far the most exciting performances come from the altos, Jones and Kuhlmann, as Ruggiero and Bradamante. In the subsidiary part of Morgana, Alcina's sister, Harrhy sings with her customary command of Handelian style. Hickox conducts with suitable flair.

Christoph Willibald Gluck (1714–87)

Orfeo ed Euridice. Marjanne Kweksilber (Euridice), Magdalena Faliewicz (Amor), René Jacobs (Orfeo), Ghent Collegium Vocale, Petite Bande, Sigiswald Kuijken. (Accent ACC 48223/4D)

Orphée et Eurydice. Barbara Hendricks (Eurydice), Brigitte Fournier (L'Amour), Anne Sofie von Otter (Orphée), Monteverdi Ch, Lyon Opéra O/John Eliot Gardiner. (EMI CDS7 49834-2)

Gluck's most famous opera, a setting of the Orpheus legend, exists in various forms stretching from the original, lean version of 1762 (originally with a castrato hero) composed for Vienna, through the longer Paris version in French, with ballet, of 1774, to Berlioz's conflation devised for Pauline Viardot in 1859. In all Gluck moved away from the long arias and strict formality of his predecessors towards a style based on the essentials of dramatic continuity and direct expression.

The first recording listed here is of the 1762 original, the second of something approaching the Berlioz edition (which, to complicate matters, was published by Ricordi in 1889, with still further changes, to become for many years the opera house standard). Most commentators now favour the tautness and focus of the original, which is well served by the Kuijken performance, graced by the flexible, tender singing of Jacobs in the title role, and period instruments. The EMI set, which includes the later, more elaborate music written for Paris, is also notable for its Orpheus: von Otter sings with all her customary command of style, tone, phrasing and word. Gardiner is a more positive conductor than Kuijken, intent on conveying the immediacy of the great work. By the way, he has recorded the original version, a set that should be worth consideration.

Recommended alternatives: Hartmut Haenchen (Capriccio) – this account of the 1762 version is notable for Jochen Kowalski's lovely singing of Orpheus's music. The set derives from the unusual staging of Berlin's Komische Oper, also seen in London, in which Kowalski starred. It uses modern instruments and includes in an appendix the Dance of the Furies and Dance of the Blessed Spirits written for Paris. Hans Rosbaud (Philips) – this classic set of the 1774 Paris version has Léopold Simoneau as an affecting Orpheus: it should be reissued on CD.

Alceste. Jessye Norman (Alceste), Nicolai Gedda (Admète), Robert Gambill (Evandre), Tom Krause (High Priest), Siegmund Nimsgern (Hercule), Bernd Weikl (Apollon), Bavarian Radio Ch and Symphony O/Serge Baudo. (Orfeo CO27823F)

This piece, like *Orfeo*, exists in more than one version. In this case the differences are so great that each amounts to a different work – the *tragedia per musica* written for Vienna in 1767 to a libretto by Calzabigi, and the *tragédie-lyrique* composed for Paris in 1776. On the whole the French work is the more daring, the more innovatory and therefore the more exciting. Sorrow and lamentation form the mood of this tale, based on Euripides, and it is one Gluck was uniquely equipped to articulate. Most of the tragic depths of the title part are plumbed by Norman's grand if not wholly idiomatic Alceste. Gedda, though no longer youthful in tone, remains a stylist, and the support is never less than adequate under Baudo's stern direction. This may not be an ideal rendering, but good enough to convey the solemnity of a noble, elevating work.

Iphigénie en Aulide. Lynne Dawson (Iphigénie), Anne Sofie von Otter (Clytemnestre), John Aler (Achilles), Gilles Cachemaille (Calchas), José van Dam (Agamemnon), Monteverdi Choir, O of the Lyon Opéra/John Eliot Gardiner. (Erato 2292-45003-2)

This is the first of Gluck's operas for Paris, dating from 1774, and it shows a further advance in his reforms, the shape and movement of the drama very much dictating the course of the music. The libretto, an adaptation of a play by Racine, concerns the incidents attendant on Agamemnon's vow to sacrifice his daughter Iphigenia in return for a favourable wind to carry him to Troy. In his score, Gluck peers into the hearts of his characters – the eponymous heroine, Agamemnon, Clytemnestra and Achilles, Iphigenia's betrothed. It is notable for Agamemnon's tormented monologues, Clytemnestra's visionary scene, and Iphigenia's delicate arias, showing Gluck's gifts for characterisation on the broadest scale.

Nobody has done more than Gardiner to restore Gluck's operas to their rightful place in the opera house and on collectors' shelves. His grasp here of the musical niceties and closeknit forms of Gluck's mature style are masterly, and he has the added gift of being able to convey his own dedication to the forces before him. He could hardly have a better cast. Dawson is a soft-grained, affecting Iphigenia, van Dam a nobly agonised Agamemnon, von Otter an urgent, beseeching Clytemnestra, Aler an appropriately heroic lover. Choir and orchestra perform with fervour, completing one's pleasure in this well-engineered set.

> *Iphigénie en Tauride.* Diana Montague (Iphigénie), John Aler (Pylade), Thomas Allen (Oreste), René Massis (Thoas), Monteverdi Ch, O of the Lyon Opéra/John Eliot Gardiner. (Philips 416 148-2)

This 1779 sequel to the above is an even more impressive achievement. Combining the intimate and the heroic in equal measure, Gluck once again goes to the heart of a given situation – here that of the exiled Iphigenia, forced to sacrifice all visitors to Tauris at the behest of the barbarous Scythian king, Thoas. Her brother Orestes and his friend Pylades, unknown to Iphigenia as such, forced to land at Tauris, are the latest victims. Pylades, allowed to leave, saves Orestes in the nick of time, but not before many moments of inner torment on the part of sister and brother. Again the action often concerns itself with the psychological state of the principals expressed in direct and eloquent terms, yet the action moves forward with surprising swiftness. Here classical tragedy is set to music which is equal to and enhances its timeless quality.

Gardiner conducts a taut, direct performance, aware of every facet of Gluck's inspiration and able to execute the composer's wishes faithfully, something not previously achieved on disc. His choice of singers is again apt. Montague encompasses almost all of the varied moods and testing *tessitura* of the title part in a dignified, compelling performance. Allen's Orestes is suitably tormented and passionate. Aler fulfils all the considerable demands Gluck

makes on his tenor. Massis is a suitably declamatory Thoas. The
recording is admirable.

Wolfgang Amadeus Mozart (1756–91)

Idomeneo. Sylvia McNair (Ilia), Hillevi Martinpelto (Elettra),
Anne Sofie von Otter (Idamante), Anthony Rolfe Johnson
(Idomeneo), Nigel Robson (Arbace), Glenn Winslade (High
Priest), Cornelius Hauptmann (Oracle), Monteverdi Choir,
English Baroque Soloists/John Eliot Gardiner. (Archiv Pro-
duction 431 674-2)

Unless and until research proves otherwise, this will be the
definitive recording of Mozart's first masterpiece. Gardiner gives
a reading that is as close as can at present be discerned to both a
performance of Mozart's time and a modern one that sounds
thoroughly authentic in the best sense. Based on live performances in London's Queen Elizabeth Hall which were evenings of
thrilling music–drama, the performance is full of theatrical life.
Then Gardiner performed all the variants of the score (some of
them cut before the Munich première) on different evenings.
Here, in the main body of the recording, is a composite version of
the surviving music for Munich, with the variants given in
appendices, so that practically all the music Mozart ever wrote for
performances in his lifetime is included.

This thorough and scholarly approach would count for
nothing were the reading not so profoundly satisfying. Having
approached the piece through the related operas of Handel and
Gluck, Mozart's noble predecessors in *opera seria*, Gardiner also
brings to the work the experience of conducting Mozart
symphonies and concertos on period instruments. In matters of
phrasing, articulation, melodic shaping, he and his forces benefit
from their previous achievements: this is a taut, raw, dramatic
reading, yet one allowing for warmth and eloquence. Throughout
Gardiner and his team recognise that Mozart conceived the work
as through-written, avoiding breaks in its momentum. This
creates the right sense of internal tension within external
formality.

Although some roles have been better sung on earlier versions, none is so consistently cast. Sylvia McNair sings Ilia's graceful, sensuous music with eager, fresh tone and impeccable phrasing. Martinpelto is a properly impetuous Elettra. The main honours go to Anthony Rolfe Johnson's deeply felt, mellifluously sung and technically accomplished Idomeneo and to Anne Sofie von Otter's forthright Idamante. The sacrificial scene between father and son (Act 3) is rightly the moving centrepiece of the whole work. Nigel Robson copes well with Arbace's often intractable music.

Recommended alternatives: Karl Böhm (DG) – the work of an experienced Mozartian, aware of the work's stature but deficient in authenticity. Nikolaus Harnoncourt (Teldec) – the first of the innovative versions, aware of modern musicology but somewhat eccentric in matters of tempo and articulation. John Pritchard (EMI) – the first-ever recording (in mono), a pioneering version using a tenor Idamante (the excellent Léopold Simoneau), and notable for Sena Jurinac's warm, outgoing Ilia and Richard Lewis's moving Idomeneo, a memento of the art of a great Mozartian tenor. Colin Davis (Philips) – now at medium price as part of Philips's Mozart Edition. This vital performance (slightly cut) features a strong cast headed by George Shirley (Idomeneo), Pauline Tinsley (Elettra) and Margherita Rinaldi as a most appealing Ilia.

Die Entführung aus dem Serail. 1. Arleen Auger (Konstanze), Reri Grist (Blonde), Peter Schreier (Belmonte), Harald Neukirch (Pedrillo), Kurt Moll (Osmin), Leipzig Radio Ch, Dresden Staatskapelle/Karl Böhm. (DG 429 868-2)
2. Lynne Dawson (Konstanze), Marianne Hirsti (Blonde), Uwe Heilmann (Belmonte), Wilfried Gahmlich (Pedrillo), Gunther von Kannen (Osmin), Academy of Ancient Music Ch and O/Christopher Hogwood. (L'Oiseau-Lyre 420 339-2)

No recording of this enjoyable *Singspiel*, a play with music (the numbers divided by long stretches of dialogue, nearly always substantially reduced these days), is wholly satisfactory, but both these sets have much to commend them. The *Singspiel* form was elevated by Mozart to something much more than mere entertainment: he invested the main characters, including the speaking part of the Pasha Selim, with deep feelings. Selim worships the captive Konstanze, who, true to her name, is constant to her beloved, Belmonte, who arrives at Selim's castle to rescue her disguised as an architect. The lighter side of the plot concerns Osmin, the Pasha's lascivious overseer, and his lusting after pretty, but mettlesome Blonde, Konstanze's English maid, herself in love with Pedrillo, Belmonte's servant. All ends happily. Mozart clothes his characters in music appropriate to each, and, even this early in his career (1782), brought them together in long-breathed and convincing ensembles.

Böhm manages both the serious and light side of the piece with equal aplomb which derives from a lifetime spent in Mozart's service. The first-rate choir and orchestra, from what was then (1974) East Germany, support him superbly. Auger makes a secure, attractive, slightly cool Konstanze. She copes easily with the feats of vocal virtuosity demanded by her three arias. Schreier is the most ardent and skilled Belmonte on disc (he also sings the role in Harnoncourt's fierily controversial version on Teldec). Grist is slightly thin of tone as Blonde but acquits herself in lively fashion; Neukirch as Pedrillo is equally vivid. Moll is the most sonorous and formidable of Osmins. The warm recording helps give this set its high status.

The 1991 Oiseau-Lyre set is cleanly but anonymously conducted by Hogwood, who wants Böhm's warmth of approach, but he does have the advantage of fine playing on period instruments and a cast of a calibre that rivals Böhm's. As Konstanze, Dawson sounds more vulnerable and therefore more moving than Auger and she is technically almost as well equipped. Heilmann is almost Schreier's equal as Belmonte – and that's compliment enough. Hirsti is a delightful Blonde, Gahmlich an experienced Pedrillo. As Osmin, von Kannen blusters with frustration. The recording is impeccable.

Le nozze di Figaro. Barbara Bonney (Susanna), Arleen Auger (Countess Almaviva), Nancy Argenta (Barbarina), Della Jones (Marcellina), Alicia Nafé (Cherubino), Edoardo Gimenez (Don Basilio), Francis Egerton (Don Curzio), Håkan Hagegård (Count Almaviva), Petteri Salomaa (Figaro), Carlos Feller (Dr Bartolo), Enzo Florimo (Antonio),

Drottningholm Court Theatre Ch and O/Arnold Östman.
(L'Oiseau-Lyre 421 333-2 (three))

This is the first version of a much-recorded opera using period instruments – and it has swept all before it. Based on performances at the famous Drottningholm Court Theatre in Sweden, it exudes a feeling of a lived-in performance, an enclosed society in which emotions and intrigues are played out at an intimate level (an ambience owing much to the skill of producer Peter Wadland). In that sense it also represents the closest approximation to the play by Beaumarchais on which Mozart and his librettist Da Ponte based their opera, one of the most popular in the repertory from the day of its première to today. It is the notable achievement of Östman and his team to suggest what a performance in Mozart's time might have been like in terms of orchestral sound (small string band, prominent woodwind), tempo and phrasing. The whole thing is as far away as possible from the kind of big-scale, international performance heard on most other sets.

A further advantage is the assembly of a cast of singers much nearer the age of the principal characters than is to be heard on other versions. The youthful vitality and light yet warm voices on display are a constant delight. Quite rightly most prominent are the bright button of a Susanna presented by Bonney and the vibrant, lively Figaro of Petteri Salomaa. Auger's Countess avoids the simpering sentimentality of many interpreters of her role, presenting a woman very much in the prime of life. Hagegård is a properly dominating, virile Count. Nafé's Cherubino is full of exuberant, palpitating vivacity. Among the smaller roles, Della Jones's characterful Marcellina and Feller's overweening Bartolo are notable. Both Marcellina and Basilio retain their Act 4 arias, cut in some sets.

An important and rewarding bonus is offered by the inclusion, as appendices, of all the variants provided by Mozart for later performances. These include a higher setting of the Count's aria, here easily encompassed by Hagegård, and 'Al desio di chi t'adora', a ravishing, longer alternative to Susanna's Act 4 'Deh vieni', quite beautifully delivered by Bonney.

Recommended alternatives: Carlo Maria Giulini (EMI) – this classic 1960s version is the appealing alternative to Östman for anyone allergic to period instruments. The cast, mostly Italian-speaking, is a splendid one carefully chosen by producer Walter Legge, and his recording is admirably balanced and natural in perspective. Available at mid-price on only two CDs it is an obvious bargain, although it omits the arias for Marcellina and Basilio, as does an even greater bargain, the Glyndebourne version conducted by Vittorio Gui (CfP), with Sena Jurinac as a lovely Countess, dating from 1955 and costing only around £10.

Don Giovanni. Joan Sutherland (Donna Anna), Elisabeth Schwarzkopf (Donna Elvira), Graziella Sciutti (Zerlina), Luigi Alva (Don Ottavio), Eberhard Waechter (Don Giovanni), Giuseppe Taddei (Leporello), Piero Cappuccilli (Masetto), Gottlob Frick (Commendatore); Philharmonia Ch and O/Carlo Maria Giulini. (EMI CDS7 47260-8)

Although this set is more than thirty years old, none of its successors is as skilled in capturing the piece's drama and *giocoso* elements so unerringly. It owes many of its merits to the production by Walter Legge, then EMI's supremo where opera recordings were concerned. As with other sets recommended in this volume, he insisted on careful preparation and rehearsal, with all members of the cast on hand, and, even more importantly, he knew how to create the sense of a live performance in the studio. This is achieved through the natural balance of the recording and the intimate, alert execution of the recitative.

At this stage of Giulini's career, he was a direct, lithe conductor, alert to every turn in the story and, with the Philharmonia in its early heyday, he projects the nervous tension of the piece ideally while never forcing the pace, as can so easily happen. Throughout you feel a positive, unifying interpreter in charge.

He benefits from a near-ideal cast, headed by Waechter's demonic yet attractive Giovanni, suave in tone, pointed in attack. Waechter is partnered by Taddei's truly Italianate Leporello, relishing every word. As Taddei himself was once an admired Giovanni, he has no difficulty when called on to imitate his master. The rapport between the two is most pointedly heard in their quickfire repartee of the recitatives.

Sutherland recorded Donna Anna in the days before her tone became occluded and her style somewhat droopy. Here the voice, true and refulgent, tackles Anna's music with keen focus and clean attack, the *coloratura* all in place. As Elvira, Schwarzkopf captures all the role's distraught side while managing to present Elvira as a rounded and sympathetic character. Her Mozartian style is exemplary. Elvira was among her most notable roles, here recorded at its best for posterity to enjoy. Alva is a graceful, mellifluous Ottavio, Sciutti a charming Zerlina, Cappuccilli a challenging Masetto, all three idiomatic in diction, which is a great advantage. Frick is a properly implacable Commendatore.

Recommended alternatives: Fritz Busch (EMI) – the original, admirably sung and recorded Glyndebourne set of 1936; Bruno Walter (Music & Arts/Harmonia Mundi) – 1940 Metropolitan performance of electrifying power featuring the unique Ezio Pinza as a dominating Giovanni (poor sound); Wilhelm Furtwängler (EMI) – a live performance from the Salzburg Festival in 1953, notable for Schwarzkopf's Elvira (in a more youthful incarnation), Siepi's commanding Giovanni and Elisabeth Grümmer's wonderful Anna; Haitink (EMI) – 1983 Glyndebourne set, well conducted, cast and recorded (a 'safe' modern version).

Così fan tutte. Elisabeth Schwarzkopf (Fiordiligi), Christa Ludwig (Dorabella), Hanny Steffek (Despina), Alfredo Kraus (Ferrando), Giuseppe Taddei (Guglielmo), Walter Berry (Don Alfonso). Philharmonia Ch and O/Karl Böhm. (CMS 7 69330-2)

This is the most balanced and probing of all Mozart's operas, formally faultless, musically inspired from start to finish, emotionally a matter of endless fascination and, in the second act, profoundly moving. Its rescue from oblivion in the second quarter of the century owed much to the advocacy of Richard Strauss and then of Glyndebourne, whose seminal recording (see below) set the piece on its move towards the popularity it enjoys today.

Although it was recorded as long ago as 1962, Böhm's classic version has managed to keep itself at the top of the list in a field that boasts many enjoyable performances. Under producer Walter Legge's direction, the singers interpret it as if they were performing on stage, but with the added advantage of intimacy for home listening. As the sisters of Ferrara, Schwarzkopf and

Ludwig have seldom if ever been surpassed individually or as a duo, both colouring their tone significantly and making the most of the text, characteristics so often missing in their successors' portrayals. Kraus is a lyrical Ferrando, shaping his music with elegance and regard for line. Taddei is a bubbling, vital Guglielmo. Steffek is a provocative, vivid Despina, Berry a worldly-wise, teasing Alfonso. All respond eagerly to the mature conducting of Böhm, whose merits comprise spontaneity, wit, and musical poise within ideal tempi, and he is superbly supported by the vintage Philharmonia Orchestra. With the help of Legge, the texture is always clear in the many ensembles, and the balance between voices and instruments is ideally managed. This is Mozartian interpretation on the highest level of achievement. More's the pity then that two whole numbers are cut and small passages are excised elsewhere.

Recommended alternatives: Fritz Busch (EMI) – this 1935 Glyndebourne version, conducted in masterly fashion, evenly cast (Ina Souez, Luise Helletsgruber, Irene Eisinger, Heddle Nash, Willi Domgraf-Fassbaender, John Brownlee) and with the feel of the stage to it, has stood the test of time and sounds remarkably fresh on its CD, digital transfer), but it is quite heavily cut. Neville Marriner (Philips) – if you want the work complete in another version that has the spirit of a stage performance try this well-cast, ebulliently conducted and truthfully recorded version. Haitink (EMI) – this set is based on performances at Glyndebourne in the 1980s and has a well-integrated team of singers, thoughtfully and warmly supported by their conductor. Östman (L'Oiseau-Lyre) – for a taste of authenticity in terms of lean, sweet orchestral sound and an observance of Mozartian style, this finely recorded set has much to offer even if tempi and casting aren't quite as convincing as in the equivalent *Figaro* (qv). Nikolaus Harnoncourt (Teldec) – this 1991 set is notable for Harnoncourt's probing, idiosyncratic, and vital reading, enhancing a lively, if unorthodox cast, in which Charlotte Margiono's Fiordiligi and Delores Ziegler's Dorabella offer special insights. Eccentric tempi are mostly justified in the event.

Die Zauberflöte. Sumi Jo (Queen of Night), Ruth Ziesak (Pamina), Lotte Leitner (Papagena), Adrianna Pieczonka (First Lady), Annette Kuettenbaum (Second Lady), Jard van Nes (Third Lady), Uwe Heilmann (Tamino), Heinz Zednik (Monostatos), Wolfgang Schmidt (First Armed Man), Michael Kraus (Papageno), Andreas Schmidt (Speaker), Hans Franzen (Second Armed Man), Kurt Moll (Sarastro), Vienna State Opera Ch, Vienna Philharmonic O/Sir Georg Solti. (Decca 433 210-2)

This enchanting performance is truly magical, thanks not least to the entirely natural recording of producer Michael Haas, who has caught the sense, so elusive in the studio, of a live performance. He and Solti were intent on assembling a cast of predominantly younger singers who would come to the work fresh and without preconceptions. The outcome is a winning interpretation that catches Mozart's mixture of solemnity, wonder and joy to perfection under Solti's measured direction.

Uwe Heilmann as Tamino and Ruth Ziesak as Pamina suggest all the youthful vulnerability and deep love of their characters. Both sing with eager freshness and secure technique. Michael Kraus's *Hanswurst* of a Papageno is consistently engaging, with the humour never overdone. His Viennese accent is a delight. Lotte Leitner, his Papagena, is equally charming. Evil is represented with a deal of fire by Sumi Jo, who dispatches the Queen of Night's arias with consummate ease. At the other end of the moral and vocal scale, the experienced Kurt Moll's Sarastro is at once authoritative and paternal. Andreas Schmidt makes a properly grave Speaker. Heinz Zednik is an appropriately preening, priapic Monostatos. The Three Ladies are sung with pinpoint accuracy. Boys from the Vienna Boys' Choir are nicely artless as the Three Spirits. Smaller parts are well cast. The Vienna Philharmonic is, as ever, effortlessly warm and sympathetic in this score. Mozart is here well served throughout two generously filled discs.

Recommended alternatives: Sir Thomas Beecham (EMI or Pearl) – classic pre-war version, lovingly conducted and with Gerhard Hüsch as an unsurpassed Papageno and Tiana Lemnitz as a refined Pamina. Colin Davis (Philips) – a lavishly cast version, finely conducted, with Margaret Price as Pamina, Peter Schreier as Tamino, Mikael Melbye as Papageno and Moll as Sarastro (again), all heard at their considerable best. Roger Norrington (EMI) – controversially paced period-instrument performance shedding new light on the piece, but somewhat inconsistent as a whole. Charles Mackerras (Telarc) – this most recent version, unevenly cast, has some of the most convincing conducting ever recorded in this piece.

La clemenza di Tito. Sylvia McNair (Servilia), Julia Varady (Vitellia), Anne Sofie von Otter (Sextus), Catherine Robbin (Annius), Anthony Rolfe Johnson (Titus), Cornelius Hauptmann (Publius), Monteverdi Choir, English Baroque Soloists/John Eliot Gardiner. (DG Archiv 4311 806-2)

For long Mozart's final opera was dismissed as marmoreal, written in an outmoded form, *opera seria*, and composed in a hurry. In recent years, its worth has finally been realised and it has entered the regular repertory. Listening to it with the roughly contemporaneous *Die Zauberflöte* in mind, one is amazed that Mozart could write such totally contrasted pieces within months of each other. Here we are in another world, one of formality tempered by the deep emotions engendered by love (Sextus's obsession with the volatile Vitellia) and jealousy (Vitellia's anger at the emperor Titus's apparent scorning of her). All ends happily because the clemency of the emperor allows him to forgive Sextus (his great friend) for plotting against him at Vitellia's behest, and Vitellia herself when he realises his love for her. These conflicting feelings are expressed in music of directness and economy, enhanced by Mozart's gift for peering into the hearts of his characters.

All this was interpreted with tautness and immediacy at concert performances given in the Queen Elizabeth Hall in 1990 (as in the related accounts of *Idomeneo* (qv)), which were recorded by Archiv. The electricity of those occasions has happily been carried over onto the discs where brisk tempi and spare textures are moderated by the expressiveness of the phrasing, both vocal and instrumental. Over all a great sense of dedication can be felt. The cast could hardly be bettered. Rolfe Johnson makes a convincingly clement ruler, one amazed at his best friend's apparent treachery.

As in *Idomeneo*, he has a wonderful rapport with von Otter, who here sings Sextus's difficult arias with vital intensity and fluent technique. Varady makes a bitingly jealous, manipulative, sensual, and in the end remorseful Vitellia, her individual soprano used to create a rounded, complex character. Robbin is an eager, supple Annius, McNair a lovely Servilia. Only the Publius is poor. Playing (period instruments) and choral singing are excellent.

Recommended alternatives: Colin Davis (Philips) – this has a fuller text, more recitative (by Süssmayr rather than Mozart) than Gardiner and a notable cast, with Berganza as a fine Sextus. Karl Böhm (DG) – a strongly delineated, lithe reading with Varady and Berganza here together as Vitellia and Sextus. Both these versions are at mid-price, both use modern instruments.

Other Mozart:
Some of Mozart's early scores yield up unexpected pleasures, and enjoy good recordings. Among them seek out the *opera seria, Lucia Silla,* in the admirable recording conducted by Nikolaus Harnoncourt (Teldec 2292-44928-2) with Peter Schreier, Edita Gruberova, Cecilia Bartoli and Dawn Upshaw, all worth hearing in a succession of well-contrasted arias, although the rival version conducted by Leopold Hager in Philips's Mozart Edition is also of considerable interest.

The *opera buffa, La finta giardiniera,* also enjoys appreciable representation in a version conducted by Hager (Philips 422 533-2) with Lilian Sukis, Brigitte Fassbaender and Thomas Moser in leading roles.

The even earlier *Mitridate,* written when Mozart was fourteen, is well conducted by Hager (Philips 422 529-2) and the cast features Ileana Cotrubas, Gruberova, Arleen Auger and Werner Hollweg (title role).

Finally try the pastoral *serenata, Il re pastore,* which features another clement ruler in the Emperor Alexander. Neville Marriner conducts a lively performance for the Philips Edition (422 535-2). Angela Maria Blasi is the shepherd Amynta (actually the emperor's son) in love with the beautiful Elisa, here sung by Sylvia McNair. Jerry Hadley is Alexander. Other, slighter pieces are really only for Mozart specialists. All are to be found decently done in the Mozart Edition.

Ludwig van Beethoven (1770–1827)

Fidelio. Ingeborg Hallstein (Marzelline), Christa Ludwig (Leonore), Jon Vickers (Florestan), Gerhard Unger (Jaquino), Walter Berry (Pizarro), Franz Crass (Don Fernando), Gottlob Frick (Rocco), Philharmonia Ch and O/Otto Klemperer. (EMI CMS7 69324-2)

Although this set was first issued as long ago as 1962, it has stood the test of time and not been surpassed, because of its granite strength. It ably projects the tale of liberty achieved through the fidelity of a prisoner's wife who stakes all to rescue him from the clutches of tyranny. An individual act of bravery and defiance stands for a universal message, all set to music of singular trenchancy. A hard work to bring off because of the extended dialogue and the change in the first act from *Singspiel* to music drama, it here receives an interpretation of total conviction based on Klemperer's sinewy command of tempo and texture, and enhanced by the excellence and dedication of his cast, all under the watchful eye of producer Walter Legge, who manages the balance between voices and orchestra to perfection within a warm acoustic. Everyone catches the emotional intensity of the work.

Christa Ludwig presents a Leonore resolute in her mission and moving in her utterance, both in speech and song. She *is* the intense, courageous wife of Beethoven's intention. Her voice, more naturally a mezzo than a soprano, conveys in every aspect and detail the emotional depth of the part. She is matched in eloquence of expression by Jon Vickers's anguished, soulful Florestan, perhaps with his heart, at times, just too near his sleeve. Walter Berry properly conveys the mind and black soul of a petty tyrant. Gottlob Frick is a thoroughly idiomatic Rocco, Franz Crass a noble Don Fernando, the *deus ex machina* in the closing scene. As the young lovers Ingeborg Hallstein (whose dialogue is spoken by Elisabeth Schwarzkopf) and Gerhard Unger are both keen in voice and style.

Recommended alternatives: Wilhelm Furtwängler (various labels) – seek out his Salzburg Festival performance of 1950 (although his studio recording of 1953 for EMI is also worth hearing), which features Kirsten Flagstad as Leonore and the unsurpassed Julius Patzak as Florestan caught on the wing in a legendary reading from the past. Leonard Bernstein (DG) – the conductor catches much of the frisson of a live performance in this spontaneous performance, with Gundula Janowitz as a vulnerable, appealing Leonore and René Kollo as a pained, moving Florestan.

Carl Maria Weber (1786–1826)

Der Freischütz. Elisabeth Grümmer (Agathe), Lisa Otto (Aennchen), Rudolf Schock (Max), Hermann Prey (Ottokar), Karl Christian Kohn (Caspar), Gottlob Frick (Hermit), Fritz Hoppe (Samiel), Ch of the Deutschen Oper, Berlin Philharmonic O/Joseph Keilberth. (EMI CMS7 69342-2)

For those unaware of its pleasures, Weber's forward-looking score should be an ear-opener. It combines melodies of flowing, individual cut contrasted with music to represent evil which was for its time of harmonic daring. The airas for Agathe and her friend Aennchen express the romantic spirit at its most attractively ardent. The solos for the nasty Caspar, who has sold his soul to the devil, as personified by the speaking-role of Samiel, represent the world of superstition and magic indicated by the supposed free-shot of the title. As a background we hear lusty choruses for huntsmen. Although now more than thirty years old, this set has no rival currently available that comes as close to capturing Weber's world of simple German virtue suborned by supernatural forces. This interpretation's advantage is an all-German cast familiar with the idiom through regular stage performances under a conductor imbued with the old *Kapellmeister* tradition.

Elisabeth Grümmer was one of the freshest, most sincere sopranos of her generation – indeed her like hasn't been heard since. Here, in one of her foremost roles, she displays her manifold gifts, among them pure tone, perfectly floated *legato*, clear diction and warm characterisation, all just right for the impressionable Agathe. She is ably seconded by the charming, eager Aennchen of Lisa Otto. Rudolf Schock, as the troubled hero Max, has a voice properly balanced (for this part) between the lyrical and heroic. Karl Christian Kohn is a suitably fearsome Caspar. As the Hermit who acts as *deus ex machina*, Gottlob Frick is in his element. Keilberth doesn't get quite as much out of the score as Eugen Jochum in a long-deleted DG version of the work, but does well enough by Weber's subtly orchestrated score, well supported by his Berlin forces.

Recommended alternatives: Wilhelm Furtwängler ('unofficial' labels) – a live performance recorded at the 1954 Salzburg Festival, also with Grümmer (in even fresher voice), is well worth searching for. Carlos Kleiber (DG) – this version, in more modern sound than the Keilberth, is slightly overheated orchestrally by Kleiber but has excellent singing from its principals – Gundula Janowitz (Agathe), Edith Mathis (Aennchen), Peter Schreier (Max) and Theo Adam (Caspar). The composer's later, more adventurous score, _Euryanthe,_ is now available on an excellent reissue of a 1970s set (EMI).

Giacomo Meyerbeer (1791–1864)

Les Huguenots. Ghyslaine Raphanel (Marguerite de Valois), Françoise Pollet (Valentine), Danielle Borst (Urbain), Richard Leech (Raoul de Nangis), Gilles Cachemaille (Nevers), Boris Martinovic (St Bris), Nicola Ghiuselev (Marcel), Ch of the Montpellier Opera, Montpellier Philhar-monique O/Cyril Diederich. (Erato 2292-45027-2)

Meyerbeer, a German Jew whose real name was Jakob Liebmann Beer, provides one of the most curious examples of declining reputation in musical history. Having already written successful German and Italian operas, he arrived in Paris in 1831, where he studied French opera. In 1831 he produced the highly successful _Robert le Diable._ It was followed in 1835 by _Les Huguenots_ which proved even more popular, appealing to the French taste for the grand and decorative. Meyerbeer's vogue continued well into this century; then his reputation underwent a precipitate decline from which it has never fully recovered. The main criticism is that his works offer entertainment, but none of the enlightenment, depth of characterisation and psychological insights that inform Verdi, Wagner and their successors. However, within its terms of reference, _Les Huguenots,_ which deals with the abiding and mutual hatred of Catholics and Huguenots in sixteenth-century France leading to the Massacre of St Bartholomew's Day is an appreciable achievement, provided it is taken seriously and that there are singers around who can cope with Meyerbeer's inordinate demands upon them. (The lack of such has been one reason for Meyerbeer's eclipse this century.)

On both counts the Erato set comes near to filling the bill. Although the work isn't given quite in its entirety (the recording derives from concert performances broadcast on Radio France), its structure is respected, and Diederich conducts the work as though he believes in it, projecting the drama convincingly and paying attention to its wonders of orchestration. His chorus (important in this large-scale score) and orchestra respond fervently to his direction. He has at his command some of the best of the younger school of French or French-oriented singers, chief among them Pollet, who makes an impassioned Valentine, the Catholic woman in love with the Huguenot nobleman Raoul de Nangis. His high-lying and technically demanding part is finely encompassed by Leech, an American tenor on the road to greater fame. The beautiful and flirtatious French Queen, Marguerite de Valois, has one cruelly demanding scene (which includes a bathing episode, very daring in its day) in Act 2 and then virtually quits the scene. Raphanel has the wherewithal to take on Meyerbeer, but her tone cannot be said to be ingratiating. As the implacable Huguenot, Marcel, whose music is suitably plain and unvarnished, Ghiuselev is imposing but rough-hewn. Borst is ideal as Urbain, the cheeky page, a model for Verdi's Oscar in *Un ballo in maschera* (qv). Cachemaille is airy and typically Gallic in timbre as the womanising Nevers. The recording is excellent, except for some variations in level. As a whole the set does a badly needed job of restoration for Meyerbeer.

Recommended alternative: Richard Bonynge (Decca) – this set has two distinct advantages over the Erato: the highly accomplished and attractive Marguerite of Sutherland and the completeness of the text, which includes Urbain's second aria, written by Meyerbeer for a specific singer later in the opera's career, but as a whole it does not convey the same sense of authenticity and it is not as well conducted as the Erato.

Gioacchino Rossini (1792–1868)

Il Barbiere di Siviglia. Maria Callas (Rosina), Gabriella (Cart-uran Berta), Luigi Alva (Count Almaviva), Tito Gobbi (Figaro), Fritz Ollendorff (Doctor Bartolo), Nicola Zaccaria (Don Basilio), Philharmonia Ch and O/Alceo Galliera. (EMI CDS7 47634-8)

This score has always been the most popular of Rossini's operas, loved and renowned for its high spirits, melodic invention and zippy rhythms. For years, it virtually represented the composer in the repertory. Happily times have, in that respect, changed, but the re-discovery of other Rossini hasn't diminished love for this consistently inspired piece.

For sheer high spirits and sense of Rossinian fun, this 1959 set has yet to be surpassed except with regard to authenticity. Callas is to the life the insinuating, wilful yet joyous Rosina of the composer's imagining, Gobbi the scheming boisterous Figaro intended. Callas exhibits wit and guile in equal measure, and her voice is of just the right weight and tone for the role, mezzo-ish but with agility at the top. Gobbi's flexible, firm baritone is a delight to hear. Apart and together, they sing with a wonderful brio, relishing words, making the most of Rossini's florid writing. Luigi Alva was *the* Rossini tenor of his day, singing sweetly and fluently. In support is the oily, characterful Basilio of Zaccaria and Ollendorff's rotund Bartolo. Galliera's conducting is unobtrusively excellent, Walter Legge's production exemplary.

Recommended alternatives: Neville Marriner (Philips) – a trim theatrical account of the score, in modern sound and observing the details of the cleaned-up score with Agnes Baltsa and Thomas Allen admirable in the central roles, though not as idiomatic as Callas and Gobbi. Vittorio Gui (EMI) – a Glyndebourne performance of 1962, with Victoria de los Angeles brought into the cast to give it added class. Her gently smiling performance is seconded by Gui's euphonious conducting. Sesto Bruscantini is the bubbling Figaro, Alva once again a pleasing Almaviva. Giuseppe Patanè (Decca) – a scrupulously prepared and recorded version, featuring the young and delightful mezzo Cecilia Bartoli as Rosina, but otherwise vocally undistinguished.

La Cenerentola. Emilia Ravaglia (Clorinda), Marilyn Schmiege (Tisbe), Lucia Valentini Terrani (Angelina), Francisco Araiza (Ramiro), Domenico Trimarchi (Dandini), Alessandro Corbelli (Alidoro), Enzo Dara (Don Magnifico), West German Radio Ch, Capella Coloniensis/Gabriele Ferro. (Sony CD-46433)

In many ways this is Rossini's most attractive opera, combining as it does his ebullient *buffo* style with a vein of sentiment for which he is not often given credit. Based on the Cinderella legend, it presents the down-trodden Angelina, known as Cenerentola (Cinderella), in appealing terms, her music at once tender and warm-hearted. At the same time the singer of the central role is called on to execute Rossini's often very florid writing for the character. Lucia Valentini Terrani has been one of the foremost exponents of Rossini's parts for mezzo-soprano in recent years, and here gives an appealingly dark-grained and lustrous account of this role, shaping her music with loving care and dispatching the *fioriture* without a blemish. Particularly successful is her singing of Cenerentola's *rondo* at the end, where she forgives her appalling sister and tetchy father, Don Magnifico.

As her Prince Charming, Ramiro, Francisco Araiza sings with the fluency and mellifluous tone for which he is famed in both Mozart and Rossini. As his servant, Dandini, who spends the first half of the opera disguised as the Prince, Domenico Trimarchi, a Rossini specialist, sings with appropriate relish – as does Enzo Dara, as a larger-than-life Don Magnifico. In what amounts to the fairy godfather part of Alidoro, the Prince's tutor, Alessandro Corbelli is part of a cast that is happily heavily oriented towards Italian speakers. Ferro, an experienced Rossinian, conducts the whole work with a care for a balance between fun and sentiment.

Recommended alternative: Claudio Abbado (DG) – this older (1970s) version has a smoother-voiced Cenerentola in Teresa Berganza and rewarding performances from an earlier, equally idiomatic group of Rossinians, but Abbado's conducting wants the smiling countenance found in Ferro's direction. The version under Marriner isn't competitive because it takes three CDs against its rivals' two.

Le Comte Ory. Sumi Jo (Comtesse Adèle), Diana Montague (Isolier), Raquel Pierotti (Ragonde), Maryse Castets (Alice), John Aler (Comte Ory), Gino Quilico (Raimbaud), Gilles Cachemaille (Le Gouverneur), Lyon Opéra Ch and O/John Eliot Gardiner. (Philips 422 406-2)

Rossini's final comedy had its première in 1828, a year before his last opera of all, *Guillaume Tell* (qv). It was severely neglected until Glyndebourne revived it in the 1950s, a production from which the first recording derived (see below). Those accustomed until then to the Rossini of his *buffo* comedies written earlier in his career were surprised at the vein of appealing sentiment that here tempers the fun and looks forward to the romantic era in opera. This is most potently felt in the lovely trio near the end of the opera. The story of the lecherous Count Ory and his adherents attacking the virtue of Countess Adèle and her companions by disguising themselves as nuns while the ladies' husbands are away at the Crusades gives Rossini plenty of opportunities for employing his gifts for musical ingenuity, and the score is one of his most delightful conceits – especially when sung and played as well as it is on this set.

Based on a successful staging at the Lyon Opéra, the recording is full of theatrical life under John Eliot Gardiner's watchful eye and alert beat, and, as ever, he infects his excellent cast with his own enthusiasm. As is his custom in all his work, he gives the opera in an authentic and complete edition. As the ebullient, libidinous Ory, John Aler revels in a role that lies high even for a light tenor of his kind and bristles with technical challenges. He remains unfailingly musical and unruffled throughout. So does the admirable Korean-born soprano Sumi Jo in the almost as demanding role of the Countess. She proves herself perfectly equipped to encompass the Rossinian *fioriture* while maintaining a fresh and attractive tone. Gino Quilico is admirable as Ory's sidekick Raimbaud and Gilles Cachemaille dispatches the Tutor's awkward aria (often omitted) with gusto. Everyone contributes to the tight ensemble, especially in the long Act 1 finale. Here refinement and exhilaration are perfectly combined both in the music and its execution.

Recommended alternatives: Vittorio Gui (EMI) – this Glyndebourne version has yet to appear on CD. Should it do so, it would be a possible rival to the above if only for the brio and lightness of Gui's conducting.

> *Guillaume Tell.* Mady Mesplé (Jemmy), Montserrat Caballé (Mathilde), Jocelyne Taillon (Edwige), Nicolai Gedda (Arnold), Gabriel Bacquier (William Tell), Kolos Kováts (Furst), Louis Hendrikx (Gessler), Gwynne Howell (Melchtal), Ambrosian Opera Ch, Royal Philharmonic O/Lamberto Gardelli. (EMI CMS7 69951-2)

Tell, which proved to be Rossini's last opera, looks forward into the romantic era of the mid-nineteenth century. Conceived on the grandest scale (and almost always cut in performance), it tells of the struggles of the Swiss cantons, led by William Tell, to free themselves from their hated Austrian oppressors, here epitomised by the ruthless dictator, Gessler. It depicts, in the early scenes, a happy, rural bliss, which is then rudely disrupted (shades of more recent crises!) by internal struggles that involve personal loss and a striving for liberty. It ends with a paean to freedom, a kind of apotheosis of the Rossini crescendo. It is a truly epic work that deserves to be heard in its entirety as here when Rossini's noble (if flawed) vision comes into its own. Without this work, it is unlikely that Verdi and Wagner would have developed as they did.

During most of its life the opera has been given in Italian translation and in variously foreshortened forms. Here it is presented in the original French and with a dedication that gives it a welcome authenticity. Gardelli brings out the poise and innate sensibility of the concept while not neglecting its classical proportions. Bacquier is a sympathetic, sturdy Tell, who sings his lovely aria before the apple-shooting incident, 'Sois immobile', with true eloquence. Caballé is here at her sensuous, sweet-toned best as Mathilde, daughter of the hated house of Habsburg, but dedicated to the Swiss cause because her father has been killed by the tyrant Gessler. Gedda fulfils most of the vocal demands placed on the interpreter of the fervent, heroic role of Arnold that looks forward to tenor parts in Verdi's operas. Most of the secondary parts are taken idiomatically. The choral and orchestral contributions are well integrated.

Recommended alternatives: Riccardo Chailly (Decca) – more full-blooded, Italianate performance with Pavarotti as Arnold. Riccardo Muti (EMI) – recording of a live performance (complete) at La Scala, fiery and immediate but, apart from Cheryl Studer's lovely Mathilde, patchily sung.

Other Rossini:
Rossini wrote an appreciable number of works in both his Italian and French periods (some already discussed) that have been neglected until recent times, when an upturn in Rossini scholarship and the initiation of the Rossini Festival at his home town of Pesaro on the Adriatic have provided his works with a welcome renaissance. Singers have come forth to execute music with a vocal line calling for considerable flexibility.

Tancredi is the earliest of these works to reconnoitre. It has an excellent recording (CBS/Sony) with Marilyn Horne, queen of Rossini mezzos, as the hero Tancredi and the delightful Lella Cuberli as his beloved Amenaide. This skilled *opera semiseria* is finely conducted by Ralf Weikert.

The recording of the light comedy, *Il Turco in Italia*, (CBS/Sony) has Montserrat Caballé as the minxish Fiorella and Samuel Ramey as Selim. This piece was something of a trial run for the more racy and developed *L'Italiana in Algeri* (1816). This has another magnificent role for a mezzo-contralto. Of four sets available, all with merits, that featuring Lucia Valentini Terrani as Isabella (CBS/Sony) is probably the one to have, mainly because of Gabriele Ferro's lively, disciplined direction. Francisco Araiza is her beloved Lindoro, Wladimiro Ganzarolli is the comic yet dangerous Mustafà and Enzo Dara is amusing as the hapless Taddeo. The version with Horne as Isabella and Samuel Ramey as Mustafà, conducted by Claudio Scimone (Erato), comes a close second.

La gazza ladra (1817) shows Rossini trying his hand at a more serious subject, the story of poor Ninetta accused of stealing by the Town Mayor (because she has rejected his advances) when the true culprit is the thieving magpie of the title. Ninetta is saved from execution and restored to her true beloved Giannetto in the nick of time. The Sony recording from Pesaro, with Gianluigi Gelmetti a lively conductor, has Katia Ricciarelli as an appealing heroine, Ramey as an imposing Podestà (Mayor) and William Matteuzzi as an attractive but none too fluent Giannetto.

La donna del lago, based on Scott's 'Lady of the Lake', is a romantic drama of elegiac beauty. In the excellent Sony recording based on Pesaro performances Ricciarelli is a lovely Elena and Lucia Valentini Terrani a strong Malcolm. Maurizio Pollini is the unexpected, rather serious conductor.

Of the grander operas *Semiramide*, based on Voltaire's 'Semiramis' (1823), is worth catching. This tale of deception and intrigue in ancient Babylon provoked from Rossini a large-scale work calling for large-scale singing, which it receives on the Decca recording under Richard Bonynge, with Sutherland in the title role and Horne as her son Arsace.

Finally *Il viaggio a Reims* (1825), an occasional piece, written as a lavish entertainment for the Coronation of Charles X in Paris, is full of delightful arias, some of them taken over in *Comte Ory* (qv). It has a superb recording based on performances at Pesaro in 1984, conducted by Claudio Abbado, that proved a revelation (DG). The cast includes such Rossini specialists as Ricciarelli, Cecilia Gasdia, Cuberli, Valentini Terrani, Araiza, Enzo Dara, Ramey and Ruggero Raimondi all vying with each other in Rossini execution. Don't miss it.

Gaetano Donizetti (1797–1848)

Lucia di Lammermoor. Maria Callas (Lucia), Luisa Villa (Alisa), Giuseppe di Stefano (Edgardo), Giuseppe Zampieri (Arturo), Mario Carlin (Normanno), Rolando Panerai (Enrico), Nicola Zaccaria (Raimondo), Ch and O of La Scala, Milan/Herbert von Karajan. (EMI CMS7 63631-2)

Donizetti's opera based on Sir Walter Scott's novel 'The Bride of Lammermoor' is the most often played of his serious operas. The title role has attracted prima donnas of all kinds. During the early part of this century it was acquired by *coloratura* sopranos; Maria Callas restored it to the range of a *spinto* who has a flexible enough technique to encompass the more florid sides of the part. She recorded the part twice in the studio (in 1953 and 1959), but her most compelling performance was recorded live when the company of La Scala visited Berlin in 1955. The alchemy between Callas and Karajan produced one of those memorable evenings in the opera house when everyone seems inspired to give of their very best. From start to finish Callas produces sounds apt to poor Lucy, forced to marry against her will and going mad after she has killed her husband leaving her true lover Edgardo distraught. From her opening aria through her duets with Edgardo and her implacable brother Enrico to her extended mad scene, Callas fills Donizetti's limpid music with equally limpid tone. Here her portrayal was more fragile and delicate, less melancholic than in the two EMI sets conducted by Serafin. Karajan exalts Donizetti's score above its usual station, making the most of his refined orchestration and giving dramatic impetus to the ensembles. Such is the enthusiasm engendered that the famous Sextet has to be given an encore.

Di Stefano is in his best form, singing with even more than his customary buoyancy and ardour. Panerai is a properly incisive Enrico, even if he sometimes strays from the printed note. Zaccaria is a suitably grave Raimondo (Bide-the-Bent in the novel). The theatre cuts then prevalent are observed. The recording, given its theatrical provenance, is more than adequate.

Suggested alternatives: Richard Bonynge (Decca – second recording) – Joan Sutherland in the role that made her famous sings with much feeling and expert fluency. Pavarotti is the fervent Edgardo, Sherrill Milnes the fiery Enrico. The score is given complete in the original keys. Jesús López-Cobos (Philips) – a recording that follows the original score without embellishments, with well-schooled performances from Montserrat Caballé and José Carreras in the leading roles.

L'elisir d'amore. Katia Ricciarelli (Adina), Susanna Rigacci (Giannetta), José Carreras (Nemorino), Leo Nucci (Belcore), Domenico Trimarchi (Dulcamara), Turin Radio Symphony Ch and O/Claudio Scimone. (Philips 412 714)

This delightful work, nicely balancing comedy and sentiment, is the less sophisticated country cousin of the even more popular *Don Pasquale* (qv); not so spruce or witty, but full of engaging melodies and rustic charm. The ingenuous, shy hero is poor, lovesick Nemorino pining after the minxish Adina, who almost drives him to distraction by proposing to marry the handsome but fatuous Sergeant Belcore. The quack doctor, Dulcamara, a *buffo* bass, visiting the rural village where Adina and Nemorino live, persuades Nemorino to buy the elixir of the title, really a bottle of cheap Bordeaux, which gives him a new-found confidence. After many alarms and excursions true love wins the day: happy end.

The score calls for the authentic *Italianità* that this attractive set provides – singers able to project the text and sing patter acutely. Early in his career, Carreras was vocally and dramatically an ideal Nemorino. His vulnerable looks and appealing, elegiac tone captured all women's hearts. Here he sings the role with all the *morbidezza* it requires, culminating in a touching account of the famous aria 'Una furtiva lagrima' (one memorably sung by the likes of Caruso and Gigli, see *Recitals*). Ricciarelli is equally apt for the affecting role of Adina, and she sings with just the limpid tone and feeling it needs. These two are admirably supported by Nucci, always happier in Donizetti than Verdi, who makes a properly preening Belcore. Trimarchi, one of the best *buffos* of his day, is a vigorous, colourful Dulcamara. Their performances are enhanced by Scimone's alert conducting.

Suggested alternatives: Richard Bonynge (Decca) – another well-cast and attractively characterised version with Joan Sutherland, smooth and pleasing as Adina, Pavarotti an eloquent Nemorino. Renato Capecchi is a pastmaster of pointed diction as Dulcamara. He was Belcore in another worthwhile Decca set, with Giuseppe di Stefano as the most buoyant of Nemorinos. Indeed this opera is served well on disc as yet a fourth set (CBS) has a most touching soprano, Ileana Cotrubas, as Adina and Domingo, a trifle heavy, as Nemorino. This performance also houses Geraint Evans's noted Dulcamara, endearing but a trifle unidiomatic: conductor – John Pritchard.

> *Don Pasquale.* Adelaida Saraceni (Norina), Tito Schipa (Ernesto), Afro Poli (Dr Malatesta), Ernesto Badini (Don Pasquale), Ch and O of La Scala, Milan/Carlo Sabajno. (EMI CHS7 63241-2 (mono))

Donizetti's comic masterpiece concerns the gulling of the elderly Don Pasquale, who is presented with a longed-for wife by his friend Malatesta. In fact he and his 'sister' Norina are out to show the old boy that marriage to a young thing can be hell. Norina's beloved Ernesto, Pasquale's nephew, unaware of the ruse, is in despair until he realises the situation. All ends happily when Pasquale yields Norina to Ernesto but not before the audience – at least these days – comes to feel that the whole thing is a bit callous. Any such doubts are swept away by Donizetti's unfailingly inspired music, judiciously mixing comedy and sentiment. The score overflows with attractive arias, bubbling duets and ensembles, and deft characterisation.

It may seem a trifle perverse to recommend a set made more than 50 years ago above its modern counterparts but, truth to tell, of its rivals, the best have yet to appear on CD, and the old version comes up new-minted in its CD form. Poli and Badini were in the classic tradition of *buffo* performers and their portrayals are brimful of vocal 'face': one can almost see them both bubbling over with high spirits while they sing vivaciously. Tito Schipa, the most elegiac of Italian tenors in the pre-war era, sings Ernesto's music with the plangent tone to which it so readily responds. His account of his solos, 'Sogno soave e casto', 'Cercherò lontana' and the serenade 'Com'è gentil', some of the most graceful music Donizetti ever wrote for a tenor, are models of style. Saraceni, with a voice occasionally a trifle edgy under pressure, is well in the picture, a spirited, individual performer. Sabajno, house conductor and manager of what was then Italian HMV, leads an authentic-sounding account of the score, but inevitably makes the traditional cuts then prevalent. That shouldn't prevent anyone enjoying a set that has stood the test of time.

Suggested alternative: Riccardo Muti (EMI) – Muti gives the score in full and lavishes a deal of care on all its detail. Nor does he, for better or worse, allow the familiar glosses on Donizetti's vocal writing found in the recommended set. Leo Nucci is a smiling, resourceful Malatesta. Mirella Freni and Gösta Winbergh are pleasing as Norina and Ernesto. Sesto Bruscantini is an experienced but dry-voiced Malatesta. The performance is admirable but lacks the individuality of the older set.

Other Donizetti:
Besides *Lucia* Donizetti wrote several serious operas that have returned, with varying success, to the repertory in recent years,

most of them thanks to the skills of such sopranos as Callas, Sutherland and Caballé.

Recordings most worthy of consideration are: Callas's *Anna Bolena* ('unofficial' labels) recorded live at La Scala, Milan, a finely wrought score splendidly performed, *Maria Stuarda* in either the version with Sutherland and Pavarotti (Decca) or that given (in English) by English National Opera (EMI) with Janet Baker as a moving, mezzo Mary, Queen of Scots, and *Lucrezia Borgia*, Caballé's first major success (RCA/BMG), where she is splendidly supported by Alfredo Kraus as Gennaro.

But Donizetti's best-known piece outside the 'regulars' is undoubtedly *La favorite*, unfortunately available only in its unauthentic Italian form with Fiorenza Cossotto as Leonora and Pavarotti as Don Fernando. Among the lighter operas restored to favour, try *La fille du régiment* with Sutherland and Pavarotti, where the great diva shows her paces as a comedienne (Decca).

Vincenzo Bellini (1801–35)

La Sonnambula. Maria Callas (Amina), Eugenia Ratti (Lisa), Fiorenza Cossotto (Teresa), Nicola Monti (Elvino), Nicola Zaccaria (Count Rodolfo), Ch and O of La Scala, Milan/ Votto. (EMI (mono) CDS7 47378-8)

This little tale of a country girl who nearly loses her lover, Elvino, as well as her reputation, because she sleepwalks into Count Rodolfo's bedroom, only to be proved innocent by once more sleepwalking, is supported by the elegant, elegiac cut of Bellini's gentle score. It is filled with some of his most affecting melodies, the very essence of *bel canto*, and nobody has sung them with such feeling, so many gentle, sad accents as Maria Callas. Whether in the *cantilena* of 'Come per me sereno' and 'Ah! non credea mirarti' or the fireworks of 'Sovra il sen' and 'Ah! non giunge' (after the happy denouement), Callas sings with an understanding of Bellinian line and *coloratura* that few if any have been able to emulate. Her treatment of recitative illumines the character from within, who is thus elevated to something more substantial than the retiring violet usually portrayed. She is ably supported by Nicola Monti as a stylish Elvino: in their lovely duet, 'Son geloso del zefiro', their voices blend beautifully. Nicola Zaccaria is a firm Rodolfo. Votto's conducting is adequate (but see below) and the recording, though in mono only, clear and well balanced.

Recommended alternatives: Leonard Bernstein ('unofficial' labels) – Callas sang the role under Bernstein at La Scala in 1955 on this set, intermittently available, and the presence of such a conductor inspired Callas to even greater heights than in her 'official' recording. Further inspired by the excitement of a live performance to glowing form in a year when she was at the absolute height of her powers, she is even more affecting than on the Votto set. Cesare Valletti is an accomplished Elvino. Richard Bonynge (Decca) – this is an absolutely complete recording in stereo, with Sutherland and Pavarotti. The vocalisation may be more even than in the Callas versions, but Sutherland lacks her predecessor's ability to invest Amina's music with a deeper meaning.

I Puritani. Montserrat Caballé (Elvira), Júlia Hamari (Enrichetta), Alfredo Kraus (Arturo), Matteo Manuguerra (Riccardo), Agostino Ferrin (Giorgio), Stefan Elenkov (Gualtiero), Ambrosian Opera Singers, Philharmonia O/Riccardo Muti. (EMI CMS7 69663-2)

The libretto for Bellini's opera about the Puritans may be an incredible farrago, but Bellini clothed it in such well-varied and subtle music that it is in many ways his most impressive work, at once inspired and innovatory. Muti realises to the full, in this uncut version, the stature of the score. He exposes all the delicacy and variety in the scoring, never allows the rhythms to go slack, and supports his singers to the hilt. Muti, at the time of this recording (1981) the Philharmonia's music director, has his players responding surely to his alert direction. For once the score is given complete as regards the Ricordi version.

In the two principal roles, Muti had ideal interpreters. Elvira might have been written with Caballé's limpid tones and predominantly gentle art in mind. The delicate tenderness of her utterance, whether in recitative or aria, and the brio of her *coloratura*, as in Elvira's moment of happiness, 'Son vergin vezzosa', are a pleasure to hear. The tenor is just as important in this work, written with the vocally fabulous Rubini in mind, as the soprano, and there have been few better Bellinian interpreters in the past fifty years than Alfredo Kraus, whose command of line, nuance and accent perfectly match the demands Bellini imposes on him. The play of light and shade in his plangent singing is just what's wanted here. The supporting singers are adequate rather than distinguished. The chorus is excellent, and the recording naturally balanced.

Recommended alternatives. Tullio Serafin (EMI) – Callas offers her usual insights, but Giuseppe di Stefano is a bit coarse in support and the score is cut. Richard Bonynge (Decca) – Sutherland is an often touching Elvira but not as interesting as her two rivals; Pavarotti, though singing strongly, hasn't Kraus's individuality in this part. Bonynge includes pieces, usually omitted, from the original manuscript.

Norma. Maria Callas (Norma), Christa Ludwig (Adalgisa), Franco Corelli (Pollione), Nicola Zaccaria (Oroveso), Ch and O of La Scala, Milan/Tullio Serafin. (EMI CMS7 63000-2)

Norma is Bellini's most noble and eloquent opera, telling of the secret love of a Druid priestess for a Roman general. It has a central role that demands vocal and emotional powers of a quite exceptional kind from its protagonist. Few in its history have encompassed every facet of the part, but Maria Callas was certainly one of them. She recorded Norma twice. The first shows her in stronger voice, the second (listed above) evinces more mature gifts of interpretation, enjoys a better supporting cast, and excellent stereo sound. Callas's performance is in equal parts commanding and moving as she sympathises and castigates her junior, Adalgisa, for falling in love with the same man and as she brings Pollione to book. She treats the recitative with notable freedom, and in aria and duet sings with those peculiarly individual accents of hers that always go to the heart of the matter.

Ludwig matches Callas both in line and expression, and sings with lustrous tone. Corelli in his prime, as here, had just the stentorian power required by Bellini's writing for the callous

Pollione and sings handsomely. Zaccaria intones Oroveso's pronouncements with the vigour they need. Serafin, always a master of Bellinian *cantilena*, directs an authoritative performance, even though he makes the cuts always made in the theatre until recent times. The forces of La Scala perform faithfully for him.

Suggested alternatives: Richard Bonynge I (Decca) – if you want the score complete and in the 'right' keys, this must be your version, but in dramatic terms it fails to match the main recommendation. Marilyn Horne is an excellent Adalgisa. Bonynge II (Decca) – in this later set, Sutherland is in unhappy voice, but is joined by a soprano (rather than a mezzo) Adalgisa as Bellini intended and she is no less a singer than Montserrat Caballé. Pavarotti is an excellent Pollione.

Hector Berlioz (1803–69)

Les Troyens. Berit Lindholm (Cassandra), Josephine Veasey (Dido), Anne Howells (Ascanius), Heather Begg (Anna), Jon Vickers (Aeneas), Ian Partridge (Iopas), Ryland Davies (Hylas), Peter Glossop (Chorebus), Roger Soyer (Narbal), Anthony Raffell (Panthus), Pierre Thau (Priam, Mercury, a Trojan soldier), Dennis Wicks (Ghost of Hector). Wandsworth School Boys' Choir, Ch and O of the Royal Opera House, Covent Garden/Colin Davis. (Philips 416 432-2)

Berlioz's grand epic was never performed as he wanted during his lifetime. Indeed it was not given professionally in anything like its full and authentic form until Rafael Kubelik gave it in 1957 at Covent Garden, where the tradition of playing it virtually complete continued in the era of that notable Berliozian, Colin Davis. His wholly complete recording resulted from his revival of the work at the Royal Opera in 1969. It fully confirmed the stature of the composer and of his fervent advocate, Davis, whose identification with the melos of Berlioz's writing is evident throughout. Indeed Davis fired his team to simulate the frisson always so evident in his readings in the theatre. The work itself may not have the most lucid or the most convincing of forms over its two huge parts – 'The Taking of Troy' and 'The Trojans at

Carthage' (much the longer) – but the cumulative effect of Berlioz's visionary concept is hugely impressive. His magnificent writing for voices and orchestra is at one moment large in scale, at the next intimate and lyrical. The power of Cassandra's unheeded warning and her suicide with the women of Troy in Part 1, the long sequence leading to the wonderful love duet in Part 2 and Dido's death scene, once seen and heard, remain indelibly in the mind.

Here Davis realises the inspiration of the score to the full, helped by Veasey and Vickers who often sang opposite each other on stage under his direction. She is by turns commanding, tender and tragic, he romantic and heroic in timbre, not least in his tortured aria when he decides to leave his loved one because of a greater imperative – the founding of Rome. In Part 1, Lindholm makes a properly gloomy and urgent Cassandra, showing the largeness of phrase her role demands. Many British singers of the day give characterful support, the Covent Garden Chorus sing splendidly, and the recording is worthy of the whole project, which was under the overall direction of Berlioz scholar David Cairns and producer Erik Smith.

Recommended alternatives: As a pendant to this complete set it is worth having Janet Baker's account of the opera's final scenes. She was a notable alternative to Veasey as Dido, offering a smaller scale, but more detailed reading of the title role. The disc also houses Baker's fine account of Berlioz's song cycle with orchestra *Les nuits d'été* and the extraordinarily inspired and prophetic early cantata, *La mort de Cléopatre* that pre-echoes elements of the finale of *Les Troyens* (EMI CDM7 69544-2). Also worth hearing is Georges Thill's virile account of Aeneas's farewell on a recital devoted to the art of the great pre-war tenor (EMI CDM7 69548-2).

Béatrice et Bénédict. Christiane Eda-Pierre (Héro), Janet Baker (Béatrice), Helen Watts (Ursule), Robert Tear (Bénédict), Thomas Allen (Claudio), Jules Bastin (Somarone), Robert Lloyd (Don Pedro), Richard Van Allan (narrator), John Alldis Ch, London Symphony O/Colin Davis. (Philips 416 952-2)

Berlioz's last stage work dates from 1862. It is a very free adaptation, by the composer himself, of Shakespeare's comedy, *Much Ado about Nothing*, omitting the sub-plot of Don Juan's intrigue against Claudio and Héro. The gist of the comedy, elegantly set by Berlioz, is the reaction of the temperamental, quicksilver Béatrice to the witty Bénédict and their barbed repartee. They agree to marry only after a spirited quarrel. The dialogue, in particular the doings of the 'conductor' Somarone, can seem overlong in performance. Here a narrator is employed to foreshorten things so one can savour the sparkle, gaiety and lyrical sentiment of Berlioz's writing for which Davis is ideally suited, though it has to be said that his earlier, L'Oiseau-Lyre recording (not yet on CD) is still more mercurial.

This set is evenly cast with Eda-Pierre's keen soprano well attuned to Béatrice's music and finely matched to Watts's mezzo in their lovely Nocturne duet in Act 1. Baker is at her best in her big scene at the start of Act 2, the most serious moment in the score, and she joins Eda-Pierre and Watts in a well integrated account of the six-eight Trio just after, perhaps the loveliest number in the whole score. Tear is a capable Bénédict. He and Baker give a captivating account of the *scherzo-duettino* that brings the work to a satisfying close. Bastin is an amusing, idiomatic Somarone. The recording is excellently managed.

Mikhail Glinka (1804–57)

A Life for the Tsar. Alexandrina Pendachanska (Antonida), Stefania Toczyska (Vanya), Chris Merritt (Sobinin), Boris Martinovich (Ivan Susanin), Sofia National Opera Ch, Sofia Festival O/Emil Tchakarov. (Sony CD 46487)

Glinka is known as the father of Russian opera, indicating that he was the first to break free of Western influence and create a native school of writing. This opera tells a nationalist tale of how, in the seventeenth century, the valiant peasant Ivan Susanin (after whom the work is sometimes called) sacrifices his life to save Russia from the Polish invader. A sub-plot concerns the love of Antonida, Susanin's daughter, for the upright Sobinin, a fighter against the invader. Glinka's score is at once tuneful and heroic in its intentions, which are well fulfilled by the dedication shown in this recent recording, which is uniformly well cast and firmly conducted. The recording is well up to the standard of other sets in this Sony series of Russian works conducted by Tchakarov (see also Tchaikovsky page 90).

Giuseppe Verdi (1813–1901)

Attila. Cheryl Studer (Odabella), Neil Shicoff (Foresto), Giorgio Zancanaro (Ezio), Samuel Ramey (Attila), Ch and O of La Scala, Milan/Riccardo Muti (EMI CDS7 49952-2)

One of the most potently inspired of Verdi's early successes, *Attila* is full of immediately approachable music fired by the energy and ebullience of Verdi's so-called 'galley' years. It has no real heroes, no real villains. Indeed the tyrant Attila, who sacked Italy in the fifth century, is half-tyrant, half guilt-ridden ruler. He is shown all too trusting of the Romans he has conquered and is eventually murdered by the machinations of the fiery Odabella, who pretends love for the King of the Huns, and Ezio, emissary of the Roman Emperor, who offers Attila the whole world if he leaves Italy to the Emperor. All this is grist to Verdi's mill, and he presents the melodrama in a series of rousing arias, duets and ensembles, tempered by more reflective solos for Odabella and her lover, Foresto, a tenor role.

Muti's gifts are peculiarly well suited to the raw vigour of Verdi's early operas. He evinces the burgeoning energy and emphasises the earthy rhythms so essential to its success, while not forgetting to phrase such sensuous passages as the Prelude and the introduction to Odabella's thoughtful aria with the care that is their due. In support he has his faithful forces of La Scala in fine form.

Cheryl Studer proves a near-ideal Odabella, one with the generosity of tone, sensitivity of phrasing and bold, arching attack to cope with all aspects of the role. This is a performance of tremendous élan. The rough, yet not wholly unsympathetic Attila is sung by Samuel Ramey with firm assurance and a resolute line. Giorgio Zancanaro gives biting power to Ezio's fiery utterance. Only Neil Shicoff as Foresto is somewhat disappointing, especially compared with Carlo Bergonzi in the rival Philips set which has a weak Odabella, but a dark-hued, tortured Attila in Ruggero Raimondi. Lamberto Gardelli is just as successful as Muti in delineating the score's essentials.

Nabucco. Elena Suliotis (Abigaille), Dora Carral (Fenena), Bruno Prevedi (Ismaele), Tito Gobbi (Nabucco), Carlo Cava (Zaccaria), Vienna State Opera Ch and O/Lamberto Gardelli (Decca 417 407-2)

This is the set that projected the Greek soprano Elena Suliotis into international prominence as a possible successor to Callas in the 1960s, an artist with something of the same tone and aplomb. Sadly she proved a star that shot across the operatic firmament and quickly disappeared from sight. Still, her all-in portrayal of the evil Abigaille, a slave believed to be Nabucco's daughter, who abrogates power to herself at the expense of her supposed father, remains an arresting reminder of what might have been. It is a vivid interpretation. The part is one of Verdi's earliest successes in dramatic characterisation – as indeed is the role of Nabucco, sung with all Gobbi's renowned gifts for portraying character by vocal means alone. The rest of the cast is no more than adequate, but by virtue of the two principals and Gardelli's secure, seasoned conducting, the set is still preferable to more recent versions (though some may prefer Muti's more highly coloured reading on EMI with Scotto as an uneven, but highly intelligent Abigaille and Matteo Manuguerra as a moving Nabucco).

The work was the composer's first success, establishing him as Italy's foremost composer. The theme of the Hebrews in exile and struggling for freedom struck a responsive chord in the ear of its listeners at the time of the *Risorgimento*, most notably in the chorus 'Va, pensiero', which became, and has remained, a popular number in its own right. Some of the writing in the work is rather rudimentary, but in other places Verdi's burgeoning genius is already in evidence.

Ernani. Mirella Freni (Elvira), Placido Domingo (Ernani), Renato Bruson (Don Carlos), Nicolai Ghiaurov (Don Silva),

Ch and O of La Scala, Milan/Riccardo Muti. (EMI CDS7 47083-2)

This splendid work, based on a Victor Hugo drama (Sarah Bernhardt starred in the original play, entitled *Hernani*), is imbued with the youthful energy of Verdi's early work and the music is already closely tailored to the tale in hand – in this case the story of the young aristocrat-turned-bandit of the title. He is in love with Elvira, soon to be wedded to her kinsman Don Silva. Don Carlos, the future Emperor Charles V, is also in love with Elvira. Here was a meaty story of love and conspiracy in sixteenth-century Spain on which Verdi could lavish his already-matured gift for drama through music. The piece has had a chequered history, but in recent times it has been justly restored to favour.

Its most recent recording is as good an advertisement as any for the work. Muti is fully in sympathy with Verdi's rhythmic and melodic inspiration and – in a live performance from La Scala, where he is music director – captures all its inherent vitality. His cast could hardly be bettered. In the title part Domingo is the epitome of fiery vigour (as befits an outlaw leader) and romantic ardour. As his beloved Elvira, Freni sings her graceful music with a fine *legato* and warm tone. Don Carlos is given arias that demand the ultimate in smooth tone and line allied to acute diction, all of which are provided by the admirable Bruson, a noble Verdi baritone. Gruff Don Silva is portrayed by Ghiaurov in sombre, moving tones.

I due Foscari. Katia Ricciarelli (Lucrezia), José Carreras (Jacopo Foscari), Piero Cappuccilli (Francesco Foscari), Samuel Ramey (Jacopo Loredano), Austrian Radio Ch and O/Lamberto Gardelli. (Philips 422 426-2)

This melodrama based on Byron's play of the same name takes place in fifteenth-century Venice and concerns itself with the predicaments of the Foscaris: the elderly doge Francesco is torn between his allegiance to the state and his love for his son Jacopo, unjustly accused of murder. It is a dour story played out on a historical plane. The portrait drawn of Francesco is the first of many in Verdi's gallery of concerned fathers. He has much rewarding music to sing. The prison scene for Jacopo is one of the most original in early Verdi.

Gardelli gives a sympathetic account of this concise, appealing score, bringing out its specific colours and character without recourse to exaggeration – Verdi is always notable for creating a particular milieu. Cappuccilli has done little better than his rounded portrayal of the Doge, particularly eloquent in his aria 'O vecchio cor', where he unerringly expresses the Doge's conflicting emotions. Carreras sings the condemned Jacopo with his customary plangency and Ricciarelli, at her peak in 1978 when this set was recorded, is in lustrous voice as Lucrezia. Ramey is suitably nasty as the implacable Loredano.

Macbeth. Shirley Verrett (Lady Macbeth), Placido Domingo (Macduff), Piero Cappuccilli (Macbeth), Nicolai Ghiaurov (Banquo), Ch and O of La Scala/Claudio Abbado. (DG 415 688-2)

Verdi's lifelong admiration for Shakespeare resulted in only two operas based on his plays. *Macbeth*, the first, originally written in 1847, was extensively revised in 1865. For long it was criticised for being un-Shakespearian. Indeed after the revision Verdi was even accused of not knowing Shakespeare, which hurt him deeply. In recent times, the opera has been rightly praised for keeping the original play's atmosphere and ideas in the score, which concentrates on the Macbeths and on the Witches (marvellously delineated). As a result of many conductors' advocacy, beginning with that of Fritz Busch at Glyndebourne as long ago as 1938, it has become almost a repertory piece and enjoyed success on disc.

Unfortunately only a poorly recorded, off-the-air issue of Callas's portrayal of Lady Macbeth in 1952 at La Scala, with Victor De Sabata as conductor, exists although Callas later recorded the Lady's arias for EMI. Her portrayal captures all sides of the fascinating character as created by Verdi and is sung with just the kind of tone and imagination the composer must have intended for his anti-heroine. None of the complete sets available on CD is entirely satisfactory, but that made with the forces of La Scala under Abbado is perhaps most worthy of recommendation as it does most to capture the atmosphere of dark deeds and personal ambition projected by Verdi. Verrett may not be ideally incisive or Italianate for Lady Macbeth, but she peers into the character's soul effectively. Cappuccilli, truly inspired as he always has been under Abbado's direction, is an appropriately haunted, dark-hued Macbeth who sings with authentically Italian tone and vowels. Domingo's heroic Macduff (fine in the elegiac aria once wonderfully recorded by Caruso) and Ghiaurov as the doomed Banquo, also splendid in his single aria, are further assets.

Suggested alternatives: Muti (EMI) – a tautly dramatic performance with Fiorenza Cossotto as a demon of a Lady Macbeth and Sherrill Milnes an intelligent Macbeth, one of his best roles, but not the equal of Cappuccilli. Leinsdorf (RCA/BMG) – Leonard Warren, as Macbeth, one of the great American baritone's most notable roles, Leonie Rysanek as an imposing Lady. Giuseppe Sinopoli (Philips) – an eccentrically conducted reading but with a fiery Lady in Mara Zampieri and Renato Bruson as a tortured Macbeth.

Luisa Miller. Montserrat Caballé (Luisa), Anna Reynolds (Federica), Luciano Pavarotti (Rodolfo), Sherrill Milnes (Miller), Richard Van Allan (Wurm), Bonaldo Giaiotti (Walter), London Opera Ch, National Philharmonic O/Peter Maag. (Decca 417 420-2)

This immediate predecessor to Verdi's great middle-period operas shows him stretching forward to a more lyrical, refined style, most notably in Luisa's music, and dealing with the interior feelings of the principals. The libretto is based on Schiller's drama *Kabale und Liebe* which takes place in the eighteenth-century Tyrol. Its involved plot ends in tragedy and the death of the lovers Luisa and Rodolfo, victims of the evil, saturnine Wurm.

The title role is ideal territory for the delicate, sweet-toned art of Caballé, and she sings it with just the right gentle sentiment. She is partnered by Pavarotti, who excels in the work's most famous aria (which he has often sung in concert) – 'Quando la sere al placido'. As Luisa's father Miller, Milnes is at his appreciable best; Van Allan makes a rightly snarling Wurm. Reynolds makes much of little as Federica, also in love with Rodolfo. Maag, an underrated Verdian, directs a strongly delineated reading.

Recommended alternative: Lorin Maazel (DG) – based on Covent Garden's staging of the late '70s. Katia Ricciarelli is as affecting as Caballé in the title role, Domingo a strong Rodolfo. Royal Opera forces provide lively support.

Rigoletto. Maria Callas (Gilda), Adriana Lazzarini (Maddalena), Giuseppe di Stefano (Duke of Mantua), Tito Gobbi (Rigoletto), Nicola Zaccaria (Sparafucile), Plinio Clabassi (Monterone), Ch and O of La Scala/Tullio Serafin. (EMI CDS7 47469-8 (mono))

Even after thirty-five years, no version has appeared to surpass the patent advantages of this classic set which enshrines Gobbi's rounded, moving impersonation of the hunchbacked jester, whose japes at the court of the licentious Duke of Mantua mask his concern for his daughter Gilda. Every nuance of the keenly written role is encompassed here by virtue of Gobbi's range of vocal colour. Instead of the customary simpering *coloratura* as Gilda, pampered by her father, Callas presents a thoughtful picture of a trusting, sympathetic girl. She gives a very definite profile to Verdi's florid writing for the character in her two arias and in her duets with her father, which lie at the heart of the piece. Di Stefano is a properly free-ranging, seductive Duke, very clear with his words. Excellent support comes from other Italian-speaking singers.

Everything about this ever-popular work feels as if it had to be composed in just that way. As such it is Verdi's first outright masterpiece. Serafin, with his lengthy experience of the opera, always judges tempi and phrasing ideally. The sound is very reasonable.

Recommended alternatives: Carlo Maria Giulini (DG) – much the most successful of more recent performances with Piero Cappuccilli as a full-toned, perceptive Rigoletto, Ileana Cotrubas as Gilda in the Callas vein, and Placido Domingo as a pleasing Duke. Mark Elder (EMI) – this performance in English, recorded at the English National Opera, features John Rawnsley as an aching, committed Rigoletto, Helen Field as a mettlesome Gilda and Arthur Davies as a robust Duke. Don't overlook Act 3 (wrongly given on the box as Act 4) conducted by Toscanini (RCA/BMG), a hair-raising account of the work's final scene with Leonard Warren as Rigoletto and Zinka Milanov a strong-willed and strong-voiced Gilda.

> *Il trovatore.* Maria Callas (Leonora), Fedora Barbieri (Azucena), Giuseppe di Stefano (Manrico), Rolando Panerai (Count of Luna), Nicola Zaccaria (Ferrando), O and Ch of La Scala, Milan/Herbert von Karajan. (EMI CDS7 49347-2 (mono))

This is one of only three operas on which Callas collaborated with Karajan (see also Donizetti and Puccini pages 34 and 104). As in the other cases the alchemy produced something special, the one complementing and enhancing the other. Karajan plays this earthy score, with its rhythmic energy and impassioned melodies, for all its worth but without exaggeration. (Avoid his remake, also on EMI, where he has become blatant.) He catches the dark hue of the score, mostly in the minor, and expounds its story of basic passions vividly and with all the skill and commitment he showed in the 1950s. This is a firm base on which Callas can work her magic, and employ her special skill at evoking a mood or a feeling through her unerring sense of style and verbal acuity. Here in her golden period, she sings her arias and duets with firm, resinous tone and finely etched phrasing. She has suitable partners. Di Stefano may not have quite the metal in his tone that Manrico requires, but does provide the thrust and impulsive conviction the role calls for. The vibrant, firm tone of Panerai is just what's wanted for Luna, and he sings as well here as in any of his many recordings, most notably in his reflective aria 'Il balen'. Barbieri was *the* Azucena of her day. She performs the part with an authenticity of manner hard to find among her successors. Zaccaria launches the opera with a resonant account of Ferrando's Narration, setting the scene and expounding the background to the complex plot. Verses are cut in the *cabalettas*.

Recommended alternatives: Renato Cellini (RCA/BMG) – this set, made at the same time as the EMI, enshrines performances of classical poise from Zinka Milanov as Leonora, Jussi Björling as Manrico and Leonard Warren as Luna. Barbieri is again the exemplary Azucena. The conducting is undistinguished. Zubin

Mehta (RCA/BMG) – strongly cast version (without cuts) from the 1970s – starring Leontyne Price, Placido Domingo, Sherrill Milnes and Fiorenza Cossotto. Giulini (DG) – best of modern versions (and complete) with fine-grained, slightly too reserved conducting. Rosalind Plowright is an involved Leonora, Brigitte Fassbaender a shade overparted but strongly characterising as Azucena, Domingo again an aristocratic Manrico and Giorgio Zancanaro a forceful Luna.

La traviata. Maria Callas (Violetta), Laura Zanini (Flora), Alfredo Kraus (Alfredo), Mario Sereni (Giorgio Germont), Ch and O of Teatro Nacionale de San Carlos, Lisbon/Franco Ghione. (EMI CDS7 49187-8, mono)

There are various versions of this opera extant with Callas as heroine. She recorded the work in the studio early in her career before her reading was fully formed and with inferior support. The other sets derive from live performances – at Mexico City (1951), La Scala (with Giulini, 1955), at Covent Garden (1958) and the one listed above from Lisbon (also 1958). None is ideal in every respect, but on the whole this Lisbon rendering is to be preferred to the others, largely because Callas is here partnered by the most distinguished of Alfredos and because the sound is better than that on the version from La Scala (where Giulini is admittedly an inspired conductor). In the relay from Covent Garden Callas was not in such good voice as at Lisbon. Whichever you choose you will hear the most eloquent and rewarding account of the part on disc. Callas takes us through all Violetta's emotions – carefree, hectic joy at her party, the birth of love when she encounters Alfredo, distress at having to give him up, torment at his anger, tragic feelings when near death. By dint of her uniquely moving and plaintive accents, her unequalled intelligence and vocal individuality, Violetta's sad plight is subtly and touchingly enacted.

Kraus is an apt partner, a stylish singer with the technique at his command to do justice to Verdi's keen writing for his tenor, refined of phrase and elegant in tone. Mario Sereni, an underrated baritone, is properly implacable, then sensitive as the outraged, then sympathetic father. He asks Violetta for the supreme sacrifice, giving up Alfredo, to save his family's honour in a moral tone that may seem dated, but is justified by Verdi's intense writing for his soprano and baritone in one of the most inspired scenes in all the composer's oeuvre. Ghione is a prompt and searching conductor. The recording, though in mono, is more than adequate to savour a very special evening in the opera house. Traditional cuts are made. In the performance from La Scala, also on EMI, Giulini inspires Callas to even greater heights of dramatic feeling, Giuseppe di Stefano is a more overtly ardent, but less scrupulous Alfredo than Kraus, Ettore Bastianini an insensitive, loud Germont *père*.

Recommended alternatives: Carlos Kleiber (DG) – a sharply characterised performance with Ileana Cotrubas as the most satisfying Violetta since Callas, and Domingo and Sherrill Milnes strong, but unsubtle in support. Georges Prêtre (RCA/BMG) – with Montserrat Caballé offering a beautifully sung and affecting Violetta and Carlo Bergonzi as an aristocratic Alfredo. The score, given uncut, is erratically conducted. Riccardo Muti (EMI) – complete version absolutely faithful to the score's markings with Renata Scotto as an involved, involving Violetta, and Kraus and Renato Bruson worthy Germonts. Tullio Serafin (EMI) – this version enshrines Victoria de los Angeles's moving, forwardly sung portrayal, one of the best on disc, with more than adequate support from Carlo del Monte (Alfredo) and Sereni (Germont). *Traviata* is a piece that deserves to be heard in a number of varied interpretations. All those listed have something special to offer.

Les Vêpres Siciliennes (*I Vespri Siciliani*). Cheryl Studer (Hélène/Elena), Chris Merritt (Henri/Arrigo), Giorgio Zancanaro (Monfort/Monforte), Ferruccio Furlanetto (Procida), Ch and O of La Scala, Milan/Riccardo Muti. (EMI CDS7 54043-2)

This somewhat sprawling work written for Paris relates the story of the occupation of Sicily by the French during the thirteenth century and chronicles the efforts of the Sicilian patriots to dislodge them. It shows Verdi spreading his wings on a larger canvas but sometimes losing his way in attempting to write a French *grand opéra* for Parisian taste. At its best, when dealing with private relationships rather than public squabbles, it is a subtle, well-wrought piece. Muti, playing it complete but in the Italian translation rather than the French original, makes the most of it in a live performance. He has a variable cast, headed by Studer fulfilling practically every demand made on her by Verdi. Merritt is intermittently successful as the hero Arrigo. His tenor is a wayward instrument, but his manner is suitably fervent. Zancanaro's sturdy baritone is imposing as the French governor who is also Arrigo's father, but Furlanetto is overstretched as Procida, leader of the Sicilian patriots.

Recommended alternative: James Levine (RCA/BMG) – better sung but less dramatic than the Muti with Domingo as a rousing Arrigo and Milnes as a characterful Monforte.

Simon Boccanegra. Mirella Freni (Maria Boccanegra/Amelia), José Carreras (Gabriele Adorno), Piero Cappuccilli (Simon Boccanegra), José van Dam (Paolo), Nicolai Ghiaurov (Fiesco), Ch and O of La Scala/Claudio Abbado. (DG 415 692)

There are three recommendable versions of this work (see below), but this one deserves to be the main choice by virtue of its superior conducting, and the sense of a live performance (though it is studio-recorded), deriving from the fact that, in the mid-'70s, when this set was made, La Scala was performing the piece in Giorgio Strehler's memorable production. Concerned with troubled times in fourteenth-century Genoa, the score is predominantly dark-hued and for much of the time Verdi keeps in rein his gift for arching melodies. This has kept the work from establishing itself in the repertory until recent times when its resource and subtlety have at last been recognised.

Unsuccessful when first presented in 1857, it was extensively revised by the composer (and the libretto re-drafted by Boito) in 1881 after he had written *Aida* and the *Requiem*. In consequence it has the benefit of Verdi's mature experience in creating more complex structures. Even so the plot remains opaque: it concerns a conflict between the patricians, led by Jacopo Fiesco, and the plebeians, led by sea-captain Simon Boccanegra, who is acclaimed Doge. Fiesco's daughter Maria has given birth to a daughter by Boccanegra, but dies in childbirth. Twenty-five years later the factions are eventually reconciled when Boccanegra's lost daughter, also called Maria (but known as Amelia), comes to light. The plot is further thickened by the fact that Amelia is loved by both the patrician Gabriele and the plebeian Paolo, Boccanegra's henchman. When Paolo is denied her hand by Boccanegra himself, Paolo poisons the Doge. Out of this complex web, Verdi fashioned a score that ably contrasts public and private passions, always a favourite subject with him.

Abbado's taut, alert direction makes the most of the work's many felicities of detail while giving a broader view of the whole. As on stage Cappuccilli is a commanding and father-like figure, singing with breadth of phrase and strong tone. Freni makes an attractive though not especially individual Amelia. Ghiaurov is a powerful and vivid Fiesco, Carreras an impassioned Gabriele. Van Dam deftly characterises the villain Paolo.

Recommended alternatives: Gianandrea Gavazzeni (RCA) – a finely contoured, lovingly played version with Cappuccilli marginally less involved than on the Abbado version and Katia Ricciarelli, as Amelia, in one of her early recordings when her voice was at its limpid, ethereal best. Domingo, also at the beginning of his career, is a resplendent Gabriele. Gabriele Santini (EMI, mono) – this version enshrines Tito Gobbi's precise, eloquent assumption of the title role. It is also adorned by Victoria de los Angeles's girl-like, fresh Amelia and the most imposing of all Fiescos in Boris Christoff. All in all, though seldom recorded, this opera has fared very well on disc.

Un ballo in maschera. Maria Callas (Amelia), Eugenia Ratti (Oscar), Fedora Barbieri (Ulrica), Giuseppe di Stefano (Riccardo), Tito Gobbi (Renato), Silvio Maionica (Sam), Nicola Zaccaria (Tom), Ch and O of La Scala, Milan/ Antonino Votto. (EMI CDS7 47498, mono)

One of the most abundantly melodic and attractively varied of Verdi's middle-period scores, this work shows Verdi at the peak of his powers with a fine balance kept between the romantic and the tragic, and light relief offered by the page Oscar, sung by a high soprano. The music is by turns haunting, exuberant, lyrically poetic, and rousing. Originally set in Sweden and featuring the murder of a monarch (Gustaf III of Sweden), it had to be resited in Boston, but is often set today in the original Swedish landscape. The characterisation is unerring and offers gifts of parts to all the principals.

Many have tried to equal the cast on this 1955 version; none has succeeded in doing so. The role of the woman torn between husband and royal lover was ideally suited to Callas's gift for etching into the listener's mind the feelings of a distraught, vulnerable woman, and she sings throughout with the right passion and pathos. Di Stefano is at his most ardent and impulsive as Riccardo (*vice* Gustaf III). As Renato (*vice* Anckarstroem), Gobbi is in his element, at first warm-hearted in his friendship for Riccardo, then forceful in his desire for revenge when he realises Amelia loves Riccardo. Barbieri is vital and incisive as the soothsayer Ulrica, Ratti a sparky Oscar.

Suggested alternatives: Riccardo Muti (EMI) – a taut, dramatic account dominated by the conductor and Domingo's impressive Riccardo. Claudio Abbado (DG) – Domingo is again to the fore in this La Scala-based account with Katia Ricciarelli a touching Amelia and Renato Bruson singing generously as Renato. Tullio Serafin (EMI) – a historic performance with Gigli's attractive, idiosyncratic Riccardo as its main asset.

> **La Forza del destino.** Leontyne Price (Leonora), Fiorenza Cossotto (Preziosilla), Placido Domingo (Don Alvaro), Sherrill Milnes (Don Carlo), Gabriel Bacquier (Fra Melitone), Bonaldo Giaiotti (Padre Guardiano), John Alldis Ch, London Symphony O/James Levine. (RCA/BMG RD81864)

As the title would suggest coincidence and destiny play a strong part in this sprawling but enthralling music-drama. A blood feud causes an inevitable drift towards tragedy in which two of the principals, Leonora and Don Carlo, sister and brother, die. Leonora is killed by Carlo because of her love for the half-caste Don Alvaro who has accidentally killed their father. Alvaro, forced by Carlo to fight for his honour, slays Carlo, who murders Leonora as he lies dying. In their travels to this denouement, the principals are given solos and duets of noble, moving character in Verdi's most heroic vein. They need a deal of singing. That's just what they receive on this strongly cast performance from the late

'70s. Price was at her most impressive as the distraught Leonora, trying to escape the fates by taking refuge in a monastery. Price fills some of the most glorious music Verdi ever wrote for the soprano voice with grand, impassioned singing and seems involved in the poor woman's plight. Domingo catches all the cut and thrust of the noble, fiery music Verdi wrote for the tenor Alvaro.

Domingo was then at the start of his career (he recorded the role again a decade later, see below); at the peak of his, Milnes captures the implacable hatred Carlo feels towards Alvaro as he fulfils what he sees as his honourable task in hunting down the man who has impugned his family's honour. Giaiotti is properly sonorous as the Padre Guardiano, head of the monastery where Leonora seeks refuge. In this war-torn drama, the lighter side of things is represented by the camp-follower Preziosilla, whose colourful music is here authentically delivered by Cossotto, while Bacquier, in the *buffo* role of Fra Melitone, is in his element. Levine directs an inspiring account of the uncut score.

Recommended alternatives: Riccardo Muti (EMI) – this 1987 set, leanly and forcefully conducted, runs the Levine close. It has splendid singing from Mirella Freni as Leonora, Domingo as Alvaro and Giorgio Zancanaro as Carlo. Tullio Serafin (EMI) – this version, slightly cut, enshrines another of Callas's magnetic interpretations and is a worthy souvenir of Richard Tucker's upright tenor: he is the Alvaro.

> ***Don Carlos.*** Montserrat Caballé (Elisabeth/Elisabetta), Shirley Verrett (Eboli), Placido Domingo (Don Carlos), Sherrill Milnes (Rodrigue/Rodrigo), Ruggero Raimondi (Philip II), Giovanni Foiani (Grand Inquisitor), Ambrosian Opera Ch, O of Royal Opera House, Covent Garden/Carlo Maria Giulini. (EMI CDS7 477701-8)

This long work, originally written for the Paris Opéra, in French, but later revised in Italian by the composer, has had a chequered history, but in recent years it has at last had its due, thanks not least to the success of the legendary Covent Garden production of 1958 by Visconti, conducted by Giulini. This recording was made some thirteen years later, but Giulini had then lost little or none of his skill in peering into the inner recesses of a score that once more shows Verdi's ability to set private tragedies in the midst of public tribulations. The conflicts between state and church and the attempt by Flanders to free itself from the pall of Spanish rule are here the backcloth for Queen Elisabetta's unhappy marriage to Philip II, father of Don Carlos, the man she truly loves. Further emotional complications involve the glamorous Princess Eboli, the Queen's lady-in-waiting, who secretly loves both Philip and Carlos! These travails are set in the claustrophobic, superstitious atmosphere of the Spanish Inquisition, the fifth principal being the 90-year-old Grand Inquisitor.

Giulini controls all these strands in masterly fashion. His principals are excellent. Caballé fashions Elisabetta's sympathetic music with a care for *legato* and a finely spun phrase. Verrett makes a tense, passionate Eboli. In one of his first complete sets, Domingo is a romantically inclined, full-voiced, noble Carlos. Milnes gives profile to Rodrigo, the Marquess of Posa, Carlos's friend and lover of freedom. Raimondi is a sombre but somewhat light-voiced Philip, Foiani a lugubrious Inquisitor.

Suggested alternative: Claudio Abbado (DG) – a version including all the music written for the work (some of it cut by Verdi's own hand and here given in an appendix) and sung, with varying success, in the original French by an Italian-speaking cast headed by Katia Ricciarelli, as a soft-grained Elizabeth (as she is in the original version), Domingo as Carlos and Leo Nucci as Rodrigue (as he here becomes).

Aida. Maria Callas (Aida), Fedora Barbieri (Amneris), Richard Tucker (Radames), Tito Gobbi (Amonasro), Giuseppe Modesti (Ramphis), Nicola Zaccaria (The King), Ch and O of La Scala, Milan/Tullio Serafin. (EMI CDS7 49030-8 (mono))

Aida, daughter of the Ethiopian king, Amonasro, is a prisoner of the Egyptians. She is in love with Radames, captain of the Egyptian guard. He is also loved by Amneris, the Egyptian princess. There is ample opportunity here for Verdi to exert his powers of projecting the conflicts of human emotions against a larger canvas, here the war between Egypt and its Ethiopian neighbours. The scene of triumph at the end of Act 2 is Verdi at his most grand and extrovert, complete with marches and ballet. Always stirring to the senses, it has made the opera a favourite for outdoor performances where large sets, seemingly endless lines of soldiers, and even elephants can be deployed. However, the heart of Verdi's score lies in the varying and contrasted dialogues among the main characters in which the tensions between them are so unerringly limned.

The score demands taut control and an unobtrusive command of large structures, for here Verdi is moving away from the contained forms of his early operas. Serafin's long experience in conducting the piece is at all times an advantage. Callas's portrayal of the title role boxes the compass of emotions as she is torn between fidelity to her homeland and love for Radames, achieving an individual characterisation, poignantly sung and accented. Barbieri is a commanding yet vulnerable Amneris, eloquent in her Act 4 scene in which she tries unsuccessfully to win the love of Radames and condemns him to death. Richard Tucker is a strong if not thrilling Radames. As Amonasro, Tito Gobbi is compelling, incisive in word and tone. The bass roles of the priest Ramphis and the King are more than adequately cast. The recording still sounds respectable though restricted in range.

Recommended alternatives: Jonel Perlea (RCA) – this version houses one of the most exciting casts ever to record the work. Zinka Milanov, especially in Acts 3 and 4, sings a refined and beautiful Aida (though she is not so penetrating a vocal actress as Callas), Jussi Björling is a prince among Radames tenors, and Barbieri repeats her idiomatic Amneris. Leonard Warren is a fiery Amonasro, Boris Christoff a dominating Ramphis. The conducting is variable. Georg Solti (Decca) – Leontyne Price (Aida), Jon Vickers (Radames), Rita Gorr (Amneris) and Robert Merrill (Amonasro) make this the *Aida* of imposing voices, but Solti's direction and the recording are a bit blatant. Riccardo Muti (EMI) – this is the best of the relatively modern sets with Montserrat Caballé as a subtle and womanly Aida, Domingo as a lyrically ardent Radames, Fiorenza Cossotto as a commanding Amneris, Piero Cappuccilli as a fierce Amonasro and Nicolai Ghiaurov a powerful Ramphis.

Otello. Elisabeth Rethberg (Desdemona), Giovanni Martinelli (Otello), Lawrence Tibbett (Iago), Ch and O of the Metropolitan Opera/Ettore Panizza (Music & Arts/Harmonia Mundi MACD-645 (mono))

Verdi's penultimate opera is the culmination of his lifelong fascination with Shakespeare. Having at last found a librettist (the poet Arrigo Boito) to his way of thinking, one who could turn the long play into a taut drama for setting to music (3000 lines reduced to 800), Verdi in his full maturity set it to music with a masterly command of free structure. Melody, rhythm and harmony are carefully and subtly combined to make one of the most direct and compelling scores for the opera stage ever penned. But Verdi places inordinate demands on his conductor and all his principals, who must be actors with commanding voices. Since the work's première in 1887, they have not often been found.

The choice listed above may seem eccentric – a live performance in indifferent though tolerable sound dating from 1938, but it is more compelling than any recorded since. In few if any performances have so many of Verdi's intentions been so thrillingly fulfilled. Panizza, a much under-rated conductor (and Toscanini's coeval at La Scala in the 1920s), directs a performance of striking power and sensitivity, effective in detail and as a whole. Towards the end of a long career, Martinelli undertook Otello, and brought to it a wealth of experience in singing Verdi's music. His is a portrayal of great pathos, not equalled since, achieved through accents of extraordinary plangency and a close obedience to Verdi's copious markings. He and Lawrence Tibbett, one of the century's great baritones, had worked together closely on the opera, and their partnership is ideal. Tibbett's Iago, subtly and firmly sung, is devilish in its plausibility. Rethberg completes the superb trio of soloists with her sovereignly sung and tender Desdemona.

Recommended alternatives: Arturo Toscanini (RCA) – this classic 1948 set, also in mono, runs the above close. It, too, derives from live performances, this time a 1947 concert. Toscanini's reading is as thrilling in execution as Panizza's. Ramón Vinay is a towering and moving Otello, though a shade baritonal in voice. Giuseppe

Valdengo offers an insinuating, accurately sung Iago, Herva Nelli a slightly anonymous but secure Desdemona. Tullio Serafin (RCA) – this firm, central performance houses Jon Vickers's scrupulously sung, heroic Otello and Tito Gobbi's manipulative, smiling Iago, Leonie Rysanek's lyrical, refined Desdemona. Lorin Maazel (EMI) – Domingo, most famous of recent Otellos, here gives a resolute, intense portrayal well partnered by Katia Ricciarelli's soft-grained Desdemona, but the Iago is disappointing. Georg Solti (Decca) – Luciano Pavarotti's live, concert Otello is sung in golden tone and with moving accents; Kiri Te Kanawa is a warm, slightly uncommunicative Desdemona, but Leo Nucci is an obvious, too aggressive Iago.

> *Falstaff.* Teresa Stich-Randall (Nannetta), Herva Nelli (Mistress Ford), Nan Merriman (Mistress Page), Cloë Elmo (Mistress Quickly), Antonio Madasi (Fenton), Gabor Carelli (Dr Caius), Frank Guarrera (Ford), Giuseppe Valdengo (Falstaff), Robert Shaw Ch, NBC Symphony O/Arturo Toscanini. (RCA GD 60251 (mono))

Verdi once more collaborated with Boito on an adaptation of Shakespeare, and again produced a masterpiece. His last opera is a miracle of deftly managed comedy achieved by economic means, swiftly moving action, complex ensembles and refinement of expression, the many melodies now woven into the through-composed texture. Toscanini's famous 1950 performance (partially re-edited in 1954) is without peer for its precision and feeling for the music's natural movement. At eighty-three, Toscanini shows an amazingly youthful exuberance and the orchestral playing is rich in texture, exact in rhythm. Through long rehearsals, he instilled his specially chosen cast with his own love and detailed knowledge of the score. Valdengo is a wonderful Falstaff, ripe and flexible of voice and acute in characterisation. The rest of the cast is in most cases of a similar calibre with the young Stich-Randall a delightful Nannetta. Indeed the ensemble of the four women bubbles over with unforced mirth. Guarrera is a properly menacing Ford.

Recommended alternative: Herbert von Karajan (EMI) – this 1956 performance has the same classic status as the Toscanini – and it is in stereo. Karajan may not achieve quite the idiomatic air of Toscanini, but his interpretation is gloriously played. Tito Gobbi may not have the 'fat' on the voice the title role requires, but has just about every other asset. The rest of the cast, including Elisabeth Schwarzkopf's ebullient (though unidiomatic) Mistress Ford, Fedora Barbieri's amusing Mistress Quickly and Luigi Alva's lovely Fenton, is near-ideal.

Richard Wagner (1813–83)

Der fliegende Holländer. Anja Silja (Senta), Annelies Burmeis-ter (Mary), Ernst Kozub (Erik), Gerhard Unger (Steuer-mann), Theo Adam (Holländer), Martti Talvela (Daland), BBC Ch, Philharmonia O/Otto Klemperer. (EMI CMS7 63344-2)

Wagner turned to the legend of the tortured Dutchman sailing the seven seas in search of redemption after he had a stormy crossing of the North Sea, which can be said to blow through every bar of this revolutionary work, the first in which Wagner forged a style of his own. From the overture onwards the music surges forward with a force quite new in opera as it was then known. A few tedious passages are redeemed by the many that capture the listener's imagination, through the possessed nature of Senta's fascination with the unknown Dutchman, and his sense of doom and foreboding lifted at last by Senta's love. Their duet in Act 2, the heart of the opera, shows the intensity of their feelings for each other in ecstatic phraseology. At the same time bluff Daland and rejected Erik are also clearly delineated. Just as impressive is the magnificent writing for the chorus, in particular the intervention of the Dutchman's ghostly crew in the last act.

Klemperer's performance matches a grand, symphonically conceived reading with a blazing intensity of feeling astonishing from a conductor in his eighties. With his faithful Philharmonia colleagues he draws out all the sea-soaked atmosphere in the score and the passion and torment of the principals. At the time the set was made, Klemperer gave a concert performance with similar forces and a sense of ensemble was carried over into the studio. Theo Adam probes into the soul of the Dutchman and sings with a fine line and strong tone. Silja was always a wholehearted, tense Senta, bringing to the recording the force of her personality always evident in this role on stage. Talvela is a burly, sonorous Daland; Kozub a sturdy Erik. Unger is a model Sailor. The recording of this mid-price set is unobtrusively excellent.

Recommended alternatives: Leif Segerstam (Teldec) – this video/laserdisc version, recorded at the Savonlinna Festival in Finland, is a faithful representation of the work, securely conducted and notable for the visionary Senta of Hildegard Behrens and the still, dignified Dutchman of Franz Grundheber. Hans Knappertsbusch (various labels) – this 1955 set recorded live at the Bayreuth Festival has Astrid Varnay's heroic Senta, Hermann Uhde's superbly articulate, anguished Dutchman, and Knappertsbusch's large-scale conducting. Clemens Krauss (various labels) – this wartime version should be heard for the haunted, intense Dutchman of Hans Hotter and for Krauss's inspiring direction.

Tannhäuser. Helga Dernesch (Elisabeth), Christa Ludwig (Venus), René Kollo (Tannhäuser), Victor Braun (Wolfram), Hans Sotin (Landgrave), Vienna Boys' Ch, Vienna State Opera Ch, Vienna Philharmonic O/Sir Georg Solti. (Decca 414 581-2)

To some extent this work, about the mediaeval minstrel-knight of the title torn between the profane delights offered by Venus and the purer love of Elisabeth, shows a reversion from the advances made in *Der fliegende Holländer.* Many of the situations are more conventional and Act 2 seems to have interminable comings and goings. Against that must be set the inspired third act in which Wagner's sustained invention looks forward to the works of his absolute maturity. The score exists in two versions, Wagner expanding the Venusberg scene at the beginning to suit Parisian taste after the tauter version of the Dresden première. Once a greatly popular piece, it has in recent times become the least revived of Wagner's main operas, partly because tastes change, partly because tenors to match the inordinate demands of the title role are no longer available.

Although not the final word in playing the piece, Solti's 1971 set offers many pleasures, not least his energetic conducting – luminous in sonority, subtle in detail and full of the requisite passion in the Venusberg scene, where he is, of course, helped by Ludwig's full-toned, seductive Venus, one of the most convincing portrayals on disc. As her rival for the hero's attentions, Helga Dernesch sings with welcome warmth and feeling. Kollo offers a decent rather than exceptional Tannhäuser, sometimes rough in tone and execution, but always involved in what he is singing, especially so in the anguished Rome Narration in Act 3, where the knight describes how, as a pilgrim to the Vatican, he was refused forgiveness by the Pope. As the upright, romantically inclined Wolfram, Victor Braun sings with a rewarding Italianate line and tone. Sotin is firm and dignified as Landgrave Hermann. The production is among Decca's best, suggesting the milieu of the piece. The Paris version is used.

Recommended alternatives: Giuseppe Sinopoli (DG) – Domingo proves a splendidly virile and steady Tannhäuser, Cheryl Studer a dedicated Elisabeth in this well-presented, modern version, but Agnes Baltsa's Venus is something of a liability. Franz Konwitschny (EMI) – this mid-price set is now more than thirty years old, but its account of the Dresden version has the benefit of Elisabeth Grümmer as an unsurpassed Elisabeth, Fischer-Dieskau as a memorably lyrical Wolfram, and Frick as the most impressive of Landgraves. Hans Hopf is a sturdy, but unsubtle Tannhäuser, Marianne Schech a blowzy Venus. The conducting is long-breathed, the playing and choral singing as good as in any other version.

Lohengrin. Elisabeth Grümmer (Elsa), Christa Ludwig (Ortrud), Jess Thomas (Lohengrin), Dietrich Fischer-Dieskau (Telramund), Otto Wiener (Herald), Gottlob Frick (King Henry), Vienna State Opera Ch, Vienna Philharmonic O/Rudolf Kempe. (EMI CDS7 49017-2)

Liszt conducted the première of this work at Weimar on 28 August 1850. Although Wagner had completed it exactly three years before the date of that first night personal vicissitudes had prevented an earlier performance. The story of the mysterious, anonymous knight who comes to save Elsa from the false accusations of Friedrich von Telramund and his evil, jealous wife Ortrud provoked from the composer the most purely lyrical of his scores, which probably accounts for its being for many years Wagner's most popular opera in Italy, sung in Italian translation. But it also furthers Wagner's innovative probing of the psychology of his characters, most notably that of the pure, dedicated but vulnerable Elsa, prey to the insinuations of Ortrud, who plants the seeds of doubt about her saviour in her mind. How can she marry a man whose name and origins she doesn't know? After the wedding, Elsa demands to know Lohengrin's name – and all is lost.

In spite of the beauties of its formal numbers, *Lohengrin* is a hard work to conduct successfully because its structure is somewhat diffuse. Kempe, whose Wagner is woefully under-represented on disc, was a pastmaster at maintaining line and shape in this composer's works and conducts what remains its most compelling representation on disc. His is a natural, well-integrated and stable reading, greatly helped by the singing and playing of his Viennese forces and by the calibre of his cast in this 1964 set. Grümmer has just the warm, fresh tone and eagerness of manner to make her an ideal Elsa. Jess Thomas is a lyrical, noble-sounding if not ideally idiomatic Lohengrin. Pitted against these forces for good is a formidable pair of adversaries. Ludwig's bitter, biting, malevolent Ortrud is magnificent; so is Fischer-Dieskau's tortured, impulsive Telramund. Frick has the steady tone and commanding style to make the usually boring King anything but that. The recording has stood the test of time and comes up fresh in its CD format.

Recommended alternative: Joseph Keilberth (Decca) – this is a live recording from the Bayreuth Festival of 1953, featuring the superb chorus and orchestra of the day and a strong cast, headed by Wolfgang Windgassen's lyrical and deeply felt account of the title part, Eleanor Steber's strongly characterised Elsa, Hermann Uhde's tense, articulate Telramund (even better than Fischer-Dieskau's) and Astrid Varnay's thrilling Ortrud. The sound is above-average mono.

Tristan und Isolde. 1. Birgit Nilsson (Isolde), Christa Ludwig (Brangäne), Wolfgang Windgassen (Tristan), Eberhard

Waechter (Kurwenal), Martti Talvela (King Mark), Bayreuth Festival Ch and O/Karl Böhm. (DG 419 889-2)
2. Kirsten Flagstad (Isolde), Blanche Thebom (Brangäne),
Ludwig Suthaus (Tristan), Dietrich Fischer-Dieskau (Kurwenal), Josef Greindl (King Mark), Ch of the Royal Opera
House, Covent Garden, Philharmonia O/Wilhelm Furtwängler. (EMI CDS7 47322-8 (mono))

Even Wagner himself could hardly tell, years after its composition,
how he had written this work in a single feat of inspiration, so
sustained and unified is its concept. However many times it may
have been seen and/or heard, the fatal love story of Tristan and
Isolde, with the many psychological and philosophical undertones
found in Wagner's own libretto, exerts tremendous power to
move and disturb the listener in any decent reading. These are
both great ones. The first derives from performances at the 1966
Bayreuth Festival, a production by Wieland Wagner that probed
into the depths and heights of emotion predicated by his
grandfather's music. It was seconded by his best interpreters of
the day.

Böhm's direction wants nothing of passion and energy, of detail
and overall sweep, encompassing the whole work in one swathe
of interpretative strength. Nilsson was one of the three or four
great Wagner sopranos of the century, unstinting and tireless in
the projection of her part, yet quite able to find the warm
sensuousness called for by the quieter moments. Windgassen's
voice as Tristan, though not so strong as his partner's, is still an
instrument able to convey all Tristan's nobility, passion and
eventually torment – his Act 3 is superb. Ludwig's concerned
Brangäne and Waechter's sympathetic Kurwenal and Talvela's
sorrowful, mighty Mark all add to the stature of the performance.

Yet there are many Wagnerites who will tell you that nothing
can ever equal let alone surpass the blinding interpretation given
under Furtwängler's direction in 1952. This is a spacious, deep-
toned, incandescent reading based on a lifetime spent conducting
Wagner. With the vintage Philharmonia in its first flush of
success, supporting its conductor superbly, the sound is rich and
saturated. Flagstad had one of the voices of the century *tout court*.
Resplendent as a Rolls-Royce and with as much power in reserve,
glowing and securely projected, her voice easily encompasses the

role, though the great soprano was by then well into her fifties. Only the three top Cs proved beyond her and – at her insistence – they were taken by Elisabeth Schwarzkopf, wife of the producer Walter Legge, who made this recording possible. Suthaus is an involved and involving Tristan, who conveys Tristan's agonies and illusions in Act 3 as nobody else has done while maintaining such keen tone and accuracy. The young Fischer-Dieskau is an ideal Kurwenal, Greindl an eloquent Mark. Only the Brangäne disappoints.

Recommended alternatives: Herbert von Karajan (Hunt) – Karajan conducts a dynamic, beautifully shaped account recorded live at Bayreuth in 1952, with Martha Mödl as an emotion-laden Isolde, Ramón Vinay a moving Tristan, Hans Hotter a great Kurwenal. Acts 1 and 3 prove more overwhelming – surprisingly – than Act 2, which hangs fire. Beecham/Reiner (EMI) – a conflation of performances at Covent Garden, 1936/7, invaluable for the younger, more sensuous Flagstad as Isolde partnered by the greatest of all Tristans in Lauritz Melchior. Here Act 2, under Beecham, provides the greatest frisson. Leonard Bernstein (Philips) – the most successful of modern versions taken from concerts in 1981, with Hildegard Behrens's impassioned Isolde and Bernstein's overwhelming direction.

> *Die Meistersinger von Nürnberg.* 1. Helen Donath (Eva), Ruth Hesse (Magdalene), René Kollo (Walther von Stolzing), Peter Schreier (David), Theo Adam (Hans Sachs), Geraint Evans (Beckmesser), Zoltán Kélémen (Fritz Kothner), Karl Ridderbusch (Pogner), Leipzig Radio Ch, Dresden State Opera Ch, Dresden Staatskapelle/Herbert von Karajan. (EMI CDS7 49683-2)
> 2. Elisabeth Schwarzkopf (Eva), Ira Malaniuk (Magdalene), Hans Hopf (Walther), Gerhard Unger (David), Otto Edelmann (Hans Sachs), Erich Kunz (Beckmesser), Frederic Dalberg (Pogner), Bayreuth Festival Ch and O/Herbert von Karajan. (EMI CHS7 63500-2 (mono))

Wagner's sole comedy is a thing of joy for ever. Here he deployed his system of interlocking motifs of sensuous and complex orchestration and melodic profusion in a piece of midsummer madness set in mediaeval Nuremberg. There the cobbler–poet Hans Sachs saves not only the master-guild from a terrible mistake in rejecting the noble knight von Stolzing but also the lovely Eva from the clutches of the buttoned-up, sour town clerk Beckmesser, and then fulfils her romantic dreams by making possible her marriage to von Stolzing. Here civic pride, the follies of the human heart, the intrigues of the small-minded are all depicted in music of gloriously expansive character over a leisurely evening in the theatre – or in your home, preferably with one or other of the sets conducted by Karajan.

Weaned away twice from Berlin and Vienna, Karajan went to Bayreuth in 1951 and to Dresden twenty years later to interpret the work with two orchestras drenched in the ways of Wagner. The earlier is the more dramatic, youthfully bold and imaginative performance, the later the more considered, lyrical and better recorded. In both Karajan draws performances of rich hue and inner warmth from his respective choirs and orchestras, all of whom perform with dedication for their conductor.

Both casts are, if not ideal, more than adequate. Adam is the more worldly-wise and philosophical Sachs, Edelmann the warmer, more earthy interpreter. Schwarzkopf is the unsurpassed Eva, in her early prime combining spontaneity, coquetry and ecstasy in equal measures for a part she seldom tackled thereafter. Her 'O Sachs, mein Freund' and the lead in to the famous Quintet in Act 3 are moments of sheer bliss. Donath is fresh and sweet, but a shade shallow. Neither Walther is ideal – Hopf heroic enough but stiff, Kollo lyrical but occasionally overstretched. As Beckmesser, Evans slightly overplays his hand, but brings out all the biting humour of the role and knows every trick of the part; Kunz is free with notes but more fun, more idiomatic. Dalberg is a slightly lugubrious Pogner, Ridderbusch warmer, more sonorous. The sum in each case is greater than the parts. A sense of real opera being made is evident in both these deeply satisfying performances.

Recommended alternative: It is well worth hearing Friedrich Schorr's recordings (originally on HMV 78s) of many sections of Hans Sachs's role, which have been reissued variously by EMI and Pearl. He was unsurpassed in the part both vocally and interpretatively.

RICHARD WAGNER ────────────────

DER RING DES NIBELUNGEN

Das Rheingold. 1. Erika Zimmermann (Woglinde), Bruni
Falcon (Freia), Hetty Plümacher (Wellgunde), Gisela Litz
(Flosshilde), Ira Malaniuk (Fricka), Maria von Ilosvay (Erda),
Erich Witte (Loge), Gerhard Stolze (Froh), Paul Kuén
(Mime), Hans Hotter (Wotan), Hermann Uhde (Donner),
Gustav Neidlinger (Alberich), Ludwig Weber (Fasolt), Josef
Greindl (Fafner), Bayreuth Festival Ch and O/Clemens
Krauss. (Foyer 15-CF 2011)
2. Sena Jurinac (Woglinde), Elisabeth Grümmer (Freia),
Magda Gabory (Wellgunde), Hilde Rössl-Majdan (Floss-
hilde), Ira Malaniuk (Fricka), Ruth Siewert (Erda), Wolfgang
Windgassen (Loge), Lorenz Fehenberger (Froh), Julius Pat-
zak (Mime), Ferdinand Frantz (Wotan), Alfred Poell
(Donner), Gustav Neidlinger (Alberich), Josef Greindl
(Fasolt), Gottlob Frick (Fafner), O of Rome Radio/Wilhelm
Furtwängler. (EMI CZS7 67123-2)
3. Dorothea Siebert (Woglinde), Anja Silja (Freia), Helga
Dernesch (Wellgunde), Ruth Hesse (Flosshilde), Annelies
Burmeister (Fricka), Věra Soukupová (Erda), Wolfgang
Windgassen (Loge), Hermin Esser (Froh), Erwin Wohlfahrt
(Mime), Theo Adam (Wotan), Gerd Nienstedt (Donner),
Gustav Neidlinger (Alberich), Martti Talvela (Fasolt), Kurt
Boehme (Fafner), Bayreuth Festival Ch and O/Karl Böhm.
(Philips 412 475-2)

Die Walküre. 1. Regina Resnik (Sieglinde), Astrid Varnay
(Brünnhilde), Ira Malaniuk (Fricka), Ramón Vinay (Sieg-
mund), Hans Hotter (Wotan), Josef Greindl (Hunding),
Bayreuth Festival Ch and O/Clemens Krauss. (Foyer 15-CF
2011)
2. Hilde Konetzni (Sieglinde), Martha Mödl (Brünnhilde),
Elsa Cavelti (Fricka), Wolfgang Windgassen (Siegmund),
Ferdinand Frantz (Wotan), Gottlob Frick (Fasolt), O of
Rome Radio/Wilhelm Furtwängler. (EMI CZS7 67123-2)
3. Leonie Rysanek (Sieglinde), Birgit Nilsson (Brünnhilde),
Annelies Burmeister (Fricka), James King (Siegmund), Theo
Adam (Wotan), Gerd Nienstedt (Hunding), Bayreuth Fes-
tival O/Karl Böhm. (Philips 412 478-2)

Siegfried. 1. Rita Streich (Woodbird), Astrid Varnay (Brünnhilde), Maria von Ilosvay (Erda), Wolfgang Windgassen
(Siegfried), Paul Kuén (Mime), Hans Hotter (Wanderer),
Gustav Neidlinger (Alberich), Josef Greindl (Fafner), Bay-
reuth Festival O/Clemens Krauss. (Foyer 15-CF 2011)
2. Rita Streich (Woodbird), Martha Mödl (Brünnhilde),
Margarete Klose (Erda), Ludwig Suthaus (Siegfried), Julius
Patzak (Mime), Ferdinand Frantz (Wanderer), Alois Pernerstorfer (Alberich), Josef Greindl (Fafner), O of Rome Radio/
Wilhelm Furtwängler. (EMI CZS7 67123-2)
3. Erika Köth (Woodbird), Birgit Nilsson (Brünnhilde), Věra
Soukupová (Erda), Wolfgang Windgassen (Siegfried), Erwin
Wohlfahrt (Mime), Theo Adam (Wanderer), Gustav Neidlinger (Alberich), Kurt Boehme (Fafner), Bayreuth Festival O/Karl Böhm. (Philips 412 483-2)

Götterdämmerung. 1. Astrid Varnay (Brünnhilde), Natalie
Hinsch-Gröndahl (Gutrune), Maria von Ilosvay (First
Norn), Ira Malaniuk (Second Norn), Regina Resnik (Third
Norn), Ira Malaniuk (Waltraute), Wolfgang Windgassen
(Siegfried), Hermann Uhde (Gunther), Gustav Neidlinger
(Alberich), Josef Greindl (Hagen) Bayreuth Festival Ch
and O/Clemens Krauss. (Foyer 15-CF 2011)
2. Martha Mödl (Brünnhilde), Sena Jurinac (Gutrune, Third
Norn), Margarete Klose (Waltraute, First Norn), Hilde
Rössl-Majdan (Second Norn), Ludwig Suthaus (Siegfried),
Alfred Poell (Gunther), Alois Pernerstorfer (Alberich), Josef
Greindl (Hagen), Ch and O of Rome Radio/Wilhelm Furt-
wängler. (CZS7 67123-2)
3. Birgit Nilsson (Brünnhilde), Ludmilla Dvořáková
(Gutrune), Marga Höffgen (First Norn), Annelies Burmeis-
ter (Second Norn), Anja Silja (Third Norn), Martha Mödl
(Waltraute), Wolfgang Windgassen (Siegfried), Thomas
Stewart (Gunther), Josef Greindl (Hagen), Bayreuth Fes-
tival Ch and O/Karl Böhm. (Philips 412 488-2)

Wagner's vast epic remains one of the lynchpins of Western art,
more than fourteen hours of music dealing with the eternal
matters of love and power, personal responsibility and moral
behaviour. As far as the music itself is concerned, it is the greatest

music-drama ever penned, and the climax of the symphonic era that began with Haydn and many would say ended here, for it is impossible to conceive of a work that could be more weighty, structurally more complex and unified, or more subtly integrated. It calls for an answering concept of considered interpretation on the part of its performers so it is no accident that the three most recommendable accounts currently readily available should be of 'real' performances in the opera house (two were recorded at Wagner's own Festspielhaus in Bayreuth) and in concert (the Furtwängler). In the studio nobody has created quite the same consistency of approach: the much-admired, and pioneering, set under Solti (Decca) was recorded over ten years ago so it is not surprising that, for all its assets, it lacks a consistent approach, while the Karajan (DG) is lamed by some odd quirks of casting and sound.

Coincidentally two of the recommended versions date from 1953. The one under Krauss, which is taken from broadcasts from the Bayreuth Festival of that year, has only recently become generally available. It represents the vital, dynamic yet deeply considered view of the work at its best. Without ever compromising the overriding needs of structure and orchestral *gravitas*, Krauss gives the cycle an elemental force that courses through all four operas with perhaps just a little lack of grandeur on the concluding night. He has at his disposal a cast of singers that hasn't been surpassed in the post-war era, or perhaps – taken all round – at any time in the work's history. It is headed by the all-embracing Brünnhilde of Varnay, who has most of the resplendent weight and security of Flagstad in the role and much of the gleam of Nilsson, while bringing to it her own sense of womanly vulnerability, all expressed with an inborn understanding of the text. By her side is the towering Wotan of Hotter (supreme in the role for some twenty years), at the height of his powers in 1953, bringing to the role his warmly noble voice, a *Lieder*-like appreciation of the text's meaning, and an innate integrity that exposes all the god's inner anguish. Every aspect of the part is thus gloriously fulfilled. In these performances Windgassen was undertaking his first Siegfried. Although he was to develop the character considerably (see below) nowhere else on disc is he in quite such ringing and youthful voice. His is a Siegfried by turns uncouth, heroic, poetic, manly and eventually tragic.

Many other notable performances grace this cycle, among them Neidlinger's classic Alberich, formidably articulate and vocally a match for Hotter's Wotan, Witte's intelligent, but slightly insecure Loge, Paul Kuén's wheedling Mime, Vinay's eloquent Siegmund, Greindl's saturnine Hagen (even better for Böhm), and many other Bayreuth stalwarts of that era. One comparative drawback is Resnik's squally Sieglinde.

That role is much more ecstatically sung by Konetzni in the Rome Radio set conducted by Furtwängler, the product of broadcasts of the work, also recorded in 1953, one act at a time during March and April. Furtwängler had also conducted a live cycle at La Scala, Milan, in 1950. In some ways that reading is even more incandescent than this Rome version, as this conductor is always at his best in the theatre, and the orchestral playing is superior to that heard here. On the other hand the casting is more uneven and the recording inferior. On its CD transfers, the Rome version has taken on new life. The sound is good for its day and the playing, a few minor mistakes apart, good enough for Furtwängler to have thanked his players specifically for their efforts. His own contribution is, however, what matters most. His approach, at once romantic and tragic, elemental and profound was characterised by the late Deryck Cooke, a knowledgeable Wagnerian scholar, thus: 'His ability to make the music surge, or seethe, or melt, so that one has left the world of semiquavers altogether' (though, it should be added, no one was more adept than this conductor at allowing us to hear Wagner's semiquavers) 'and is swept up in a great spiritual experience.'

As Brünnhilde, Mödl's peculiar tone is an acquired taste, but once one knows what she is about the rewards are great in terms of a realisation of her character's psychology as encoded in the words and notes. Hers remains an individual and eloquent reading. Her Wotan is the more prosaic Frantz: a reliable, secure but seldom inspired god. Her Siegfried, Suthaus, is by contrast one of the most vivid on disc – or in the work's history. He suggests all the youth's fire in *Siegfried*, his growth to manhood and eventually knowledge in *Götterdämmerung*, and he sings with unfailing musicality. Neidlinger's Alberich (heard only in *Rheingold*) is not quite as imposing as it was later to become. Windgassen is a lyrically ardent Siegmund but a rather dull Loge. Patzak is a singular Mime – his deliberate avoidance of all exaggeration and his innate musicality give the character a more sympathetic cut than usual. The young Jurinac contributes gloriously in a number of roles. Klose is a marvellously urgent Waltraute. Greindl is again an imposing Hagen. Each part is sung with an understanding of the right idiom.

Both the above versions are available only as complete sets, both at well below full price, the Krauss the cheaper of the two. The four operas in Böhm's set are available separately at full price. His reading, taken from 1966/7 Bayreuth performances, has been described as being in 'colourful, pulsating, alfresco style' (Wolfgang Schwinger). Böhm is remarkably scrupulous in obeying Wagner's copious markings as regards changes of tempo and dynamics. He also paces and shapes the four works overall with an unerring sense of their structure and the needs of maintaining dramatic interest. If he doesn't quite offer the insightful readings given by his two great predecessors, his approach is a welcome antidote to more ponderous accounts of the cycle.

Nilsson's Brünnhilde, tirelessly sung, evinces a keen understanding of her character's development from the eager young goddess of *Die Walküre* through the ardent lover of *Siegfried* and the early part of *Götterdämmerung*, to the tragedy and heroism of its later acts. Windgassen offers a maturer, more thoughtful, equally well-sung Siegfried, compared with his reading of the role for Krauss. Rysanek's classic Sieglinde of the post-war era is expressively intense and thrilling above the stave. She is partnered by King's stalwart, often ardent Siegmund. Adam is a straightforward, intelligent, occasionally gruff Wotan, Neidlinger's Alberich is as formidable as ever. The basses are a distinguished lot. Windgassen is again a Loge who doesn't overplay the role as do some character tenors. The Bayreuth forces of the day play wonderfully well for the alert Böhm. The stereo recording catches the light and shade of the work in ideal balance with the singers, a distinct advantage over the other two, mono sets.

Any one of these versions offers a lifetime's reward in learning the magnificence of the whole cycle in different, equally valid interpretations. Try to hear them all.

Recommended alternatives: Reginald Goodall (EMI) – this cycle recorded at the London Coliseum in the 1970s preserves the special achievement of the English National Opera of the day of performing the work in English. There is a splendid group of singers under a conductor who had honed them and his orchestra to give an integrated, unified view of the cycle, long breathed in every sense and totally consistent with Goodall's grand vision. Most notable in the cast are Rita Hunter's radiant, secure Brünnhilde, Alberto Remedios's lyrical, refined Siegfried and Norman Bailey's authoritative Wotan. Sir Georg Solti (Decca) – the best parts of his trail-blazing cycle are *Das Rheingold*, which in its times caused a sensation in sound terms and is still a thrilling experience, and *Götterdämmerung*, with Nilsson and Windgassen (again) and Gottlob Frick's saturnine Hagen. The two middle operas also have much to commend them, not least Hotter's towering Wanderer in *Siegfried*, but Solti's direction, for all its immediate excitements, can be erratic. Bernard Haitink (EMI) – this as yet incomplete new cycle is notable to date for a well-shaped, clearly delineated *Rheingold* and a dynamic, finely recorded *Siegfried*. Wolfgang Sawallisch (EMI) – here is an interesting video/laserdisc version based on Nicholas Lehnhoff's eccentric, modern staging for the Bavarian State Opera in Munich. Sawallisch's reading is in the Böhm mould; it is excellently played. Hildegard Behrens is a vocally variable, but always committed and intelligent Brünnhilde, Robert Hale quite the most moving and striking of recent Wotans. René Kollo is a more-than-adequate Siegfried, a shade past his best in voice. Julia Varady is a warm Sieglinde. The rest of the cast are of a high calibre. Picture and sound quality are truthful.

> *Parsifal.* 1. Irene Dalis (Kundry), Jess Thomas (Parsifal), George London (Amfortas), Gustav Neidlinger (Klingsor), Hans Hotter (Gurnemanz), Martti Talvela (Titurel), Bayreuth Festival Ch and O/Hans Knappertsbusch. (Philips 416 390-2)
> 2. Waltraud Meier (Kundry), Siegfried Jerusalem (Parsifal), José van Dam (Amfortas), Gunther von Kannen (Klingsor), Mathias Hölle (Gurnemanz), John Tomlinson (Titurel), Berlin State Opera Ch, Berlin Philharmonic O/Daniel Barenboim. (Erato 9031-74448-2)

Wagner's final opera is the last and perhaps greatest exposition of his motif-led method of composing, here at the service of the mythical tale of the knight Parsifal. He kills a swan in the land of the grail-keepers, headed by the revered Gurnemanz, incites their disdain, and is found next under the spell of the equivocal Kundry, slave to the evil, self-castrated Klingsor. Finally rejecting her wiles and destroying Klingsor's magic power he returns to the grail-keepers a transformed, Christ-like figure who heals the wound of the stricken king Amfortas and renews the grail's power.

This neo-Christian message is expressed in music of grave, spiritual power leavened at the start of Act 2 by the delightful and diaphanous music for the Flower Maidens. Act 1 can, under poor direction, seem over long; Act 3 is inspired from start to finish, a dignified, intense and finally cleansing end to Wagner's mould-shattering and magnificent career in the opera house, latterly his own, at Bayreuth. So it is only fitting that a performance recorded live there in 1962, and conducted by the legendary Knapperts-busch, should remain the yardstick by which all others are judged (coupled with his earlier, 1951 mono set from Bayreuth, shortly to be reissued on CD by Teldec). His command of the long line, the grand, searing statement, and overall structure is plain to hear, as is the heart-searching beauty he obtains from the Bayreuth Chorus and Orchestra. This performance is *hors concours*, likely never to be surpassed. At its heart it has Hotter's overwhelming, perceptive singing of Gurnemanz's music, which he wholly redeems from any charge of boredom. Thomas's Parsifal is finely sung, in measured tones. Dalis is a thoroughly involved Kundry, London an agonised Amfortas, Neidlinger a formidable Klingsor.

The most recent (1991) version, conducted by Barenboim, has the advantage of superb sound quality, the best to date in this work. Barenboim feels the awe and inner majesty of the writing and conveys that to his superb chorus and orchestra, although just once or twice in his reverence before the score, he allows it to be becalmed. He has a superb Kundry in Meier, who is unsurpassed in this strange creature's sensuality and fury, and as upright, tonally beautiful and sensitive a Parsifal as one could hope to hear in Jerusalem. Together they make the second half of Act 2 unforgettably vivid. Van Dam is a searing Amfortas, Hölle a more-than-adequate but vocally uneven Gurnemanz, von Kannen a biting Klingsor.

Recommended alternatives: Herbert von Karajan – the modern version to have until Barenboim's appeared, with Kurt Moll's beautifully sung Gurnemanz and rewarding performances elsewhere. Try also to hear the historic version of Act 3 on Preiser, recorded at Bayreuth in 1930 and conducted magisterially by Karl Muck, whose experience of the opera dates back almost to its inception, with singers of an older school who still have much to tell us about interpreting the work today.

Other Wagner:
'Les Introuvables du Chant Wagnerien'. EMI CMS7 64008-2. This four-disc set preserves historic performances of Wagner dating from 78rpm records of the 1920s and later to the famous stereo (1957) account of the Senta–Dutchman duet from *Der fliegende Holländer* by Nilsson and Hotter. The set includes examples of such notable and, in many cases, unsurpassed Wagner singers as Frida Leider and Melchior (the *Tristan* love duet) and Friedrich Schorr. In addition, there are singers who have been largely forgotten or overlooked, such as the Australian soprano Florence Austral (the *Götterdämmerung* love duet with English tenor Walter Widdop) and Marjorie Lawrence (a stunning Brünnhilde when only twenty-four), the French soprano Germaine Lubin (a moving Isolde), the Chicago-born French baritone Arthur Endrèze (Dutchman's monologue) and French bass Marcel Journet (Wotan's farewell). Then there are worthwhile souvenirs of Alexander Kipnis's noble Gurnemanz, Elisabeth Rethberg's thrilling Senta, Maria Müller's eager Elisabeth, Meta Seine-meyer's Sieglinde and Isolde (this soprano died in her thirties after a meteoric career – she was an intense, warm artist of outstanding merit) and much else, not forgetting such curiosities as Aureliano Pertile's account of Lohengrin's arrival sung in Italian. One or two technical difficulties on CD2 apart, the transfers are excellent.

Charles Gounod (1818–93)

Faust. Cheryl Studer (Marguerite), Martine Mahé (Siébel), Nadine Denize (Marthe), Richard Leech (Faust), Thomas Hampson (Valentin), José van Dam (Mephistophélès),

French Army Ch, Toulouse Capitole Ch and O/Michel Plasson. (EMI CDC7 54358-2)

In spite of a good deal of flak from superior beings, Gounod's old warhorse continues to be popular with the opera-going public whenever it is performed. Its profusion of melody, exquisite orchestration and irresistible story, far removed from Goethe's original, of an elegant, mildly Satanic Mephisto converting Faust from an old man into a personable youth at the price of his soul, continues to capture the public's imagination – and why not? New versions appear with reasonable regularity on disc. After a series of versions that were frankly unidiomatic and/or heavy-handed, this set came as manna from heaven to friends of this lovable score, here given complete and with the addition of three numbers excluded or replaced by Gounod before the 1859 première. The ballet music is also there in another appendix. However, it does not restore the dialogue of the first version later turned into recitative by Gounod himself. (English National Opera showed recently how effective this spoken version can be.)

Plasson may at times linger too long over the admitted beauties of Gounod's writing but, by and large, he conducts the piece with the mixture of sensuousness, panache and elegance that is its due, convincingly supported by his own excellent Toulouse forces, augmented in the Soldiers' Chorus – a stroke of inspiration on EMI's part – by the French Army Choir who sing as to the manner bred. So many earlier sets of the opera have been weakened by the absence of French style in the solo singing. Here it is to be heard in abundance. Cheryl Studer, so proficient in German and Italian opera (see *passim*), proves herself just as able to adapt her appreciable resources of tone, phrasing and dynamic control to the more reticent demands of French opera. She sings the whole role, but particularly her King of Thulé song, the Jewel aria and her contribution to the Garden scene (all in Act 3) with impeccable taste allied to a sense of Marguerite's growing elation. Then, when deserted, she brings infinite sadness to her solo in her chamber and to the Church scene. Beside her Richard Leech is equally aware of the correct style, has the appropriate timbre for Gounod's graceful music for Faust, and delivers it with appropriate ardour while singing – like Studer – good French. Compared to his East European rivals on other sets, van Dam shows an instinctive command of French and quite avoids their exaggerated antics. His versions of the Calf of Gold (and its earlier alternative in the Appendix) and his Serenade are impeccably projected. The supporting cast is just as admirable. This is an indisputable best buy.

Jacques Offenbach (1819–1880)

Les Contes d'Hoffmann. Joan Sutherland (Olympia, Giulietta, Antonia, Stella), Huguette Tourangeau (Nicklausse, the Muse), Margarita Lilowa (Voice of Antonia's Mother), Placido Domingo (Hoffmann), Hugues Cuenod (Andrès Cochenille, Pitichinaccio, Frantz), Jacques Charon (Spalanzani), Gabriel Bacquier (Lindorf, Coppélius, Dapertutto, Dr Miracle), Paul Plishka (Crespel), Lausanne Pro Arte Ch, Ch and O of Suisse Romande/Richard Bonynge. (Decca 417 363-2)

The problems of performing this piece are partly textual. The composer died before completing it and nobody knows exactly what form it would have taken had he lived longer. He died after finishing the piano score and orchestrating the first act. He left sketches of the rest that were completed by Ernest Guiraud who also 'musicked' the dialogue into recitative. Nobody is certain if Offenbach himself would have preferred recitative or the original dialogue, how much of the music he had completed he would have then included in the finished product, and in precisely what order he would have liked the acts played. We can be sure that the traditional version, current until recent research changed matters, is in many ways corrupt, and contains music – for instance, Dapertutto's 'Scintille diamant' and the Septet, both in the Giulietta act – that is definitely not intended for this work, but so traditional and effective are these spurious pieces that who's to say they ought to be omitted. Compromises have to be made and, on the whole, it is better to exclude inferior music recently unearthed that adds little to the score's lustre.

Most recent versions have tended to resuscitate too many feeble passages. Not so Richard Bonynge in his 1972 set, which also has the advantage of having the four heroines and four villains all taken respectively by the same singer, as Offenbach definitely intended. Bonynge also opts for dialogue and the inclusion of some of the spurious numbers. Above all he shows a sure feeling for the brio and sensuousness that should inform any performance. Sutherland doesn't offer a very pertinent character-isation of any of the heroines, but she sings them all with care and some feeling. Domingo gives us a plausibly youthful, ardent and gullible Hoffmann, if one wanting the elegance of French tenors in the past. The happiest portrayals come from the Francophone singers – chief among them Bacquier, who is superbly malevolent and incisive in all his parts, and Cuenod in the four roles for character tenor, all wonderfully delineated. Should the famous 1948 EMI version, conducted by André Cluytens, ever appear on CD it should be acquired – it preserves a forgotten and idiomatic way of performing the piece at the Opéra-Comique now sadly in abeyance.

La belle Hélène. Jessye Norman (Hélène), Colette Alliot-Lugaz (Oreste), John Aler (Paris), Charles Burles (Menelaus), Gabriel Bacquier (Agamemnon), Jean-Philippe Lafont (Cal-chas), Jacques Loreau (Achilles), Ch and O of Toulouse Capitole/Michel Plasson. (EMI CDS7 47157-8)

This satire on the mythical story of Helen of Troy and the havoc she creates through her beauty has easily stood the test of time and, it must be said, many over-the-top performances. It is at the same time a satire on the court of Napoleon III, rather harder to fathom today. The score, one of the composer's most felicitous, carries all before it, especially in a reading so enjoyable as this one, full of good tunes, catchy rhythms, and subtle humour. Norman may not be ideally light or French enough for the title part, but she enters eagerly into the spirit of the piece. Though American, Aler has a voice with a typically French timbre, and the remainder of the cast are experienced vocal comedians. All are kept in order by Plasson's joyful conducting.

Les Brigands. Colette Alliot-Lugaz (Fragoletto), Ghyslaine Raphanel (Fiorella), Tibère Raffalli (Falsacappa), Thierry Dran (Duke of Mantua), Jean-Luc Viala (Comte de Gloria-

Cassis), Bernard Pisani (Antonio), François le Roux (Baron de Campo Tasso), Pierre-Yves le Maigat (Barbavano), Michel Trempont (Pietro), Ch and O of Lyon Opéra/John Eliot Gardiner. (EMI CDS7 49830-2)

This classic *opéra-bouffe*, first given in 1869, is a totally inconsequential, zany tale of cops, robbers and aristocrats with parodies of many styles of music, many sorts of authority, and more extended ensembles than in most Offenbach scores. The action of Act 2 takes place on the non-existent border between Italy and Spain! *Les Brigands* is possibly the composer's most consistent work in his chosen genre, and in more than one respect foreshadows Gilbert and Sullivan's operettas (indeed Gilbert made an English translation of the witty text by Meilhac and Halévy) while having a typically French element of cynicism and daring. The famous line 'one should steal according to the position one occupies in society' still rings a bell as a comment on official corruption.

The work's neglect in Britain remains puzzling. This admirable recording should do much to extend its popularity. It is based on stage performances at the Lyon Opéra with the same cast and forces during 1988, and the experience in the theatre tells, as do the authentic French accents of the singers. Most of the cast have a moment in which to shine, and they take it eagerly. Gardiner conducts with lightness and his customary aplomb. Highly recommended.

Orphée aux enfers. Mady Mesplé (Eurydice), Michèle Command (Venus), Danièle Castaing (Juno), Jane Rhodes (Public Opinion), Jane Berbié (Cupid), Michel Sénéchal (Orpheus), Charles Burles (Aristeus/Pluto), André Mallabrera (Mercury), Bruce Brewer (John Styx), Michel Trempont (Jupiter), Ch and O of the Toulouse Capitole/Michel Plasson. (EMI CDS7 49647-2)

The Can-Can ('galop infernale') made this merry satire on the Orpheus legend popular, written in 1858, revised and enlarged in 1874 (the version given here). On the whole this entertaining and idiomatic performance, employing some of the best French singing-actors of the day, avoids the vulgarity and exaggeration attendant on most Anglo–Saxon stage performances. Plasson's touch is light, with the appropriate élan Offenbach calls for and, where needed, a touch of sentiment. As Orpheus, Sénéchal sings with wit and flair, and Mesplé is an experienced Eurydice.

> *La Périchole.* Teresa Berganza (Périchole), José Carreras (Piquillo), Michel Sénéchal (Don Pedro), Gabriel Bacquier (Viceroy), Michel Trempont (Panatellas), Ch and O of the Toulouse Capitole/Michel Plasson. (EMI CDS7 47362-8)

This delightful piece (written in 1868, revised in 1874) mixes sentiment and fun in equal measure. Here is parody of court protocol, Donizettian conspirators and an absurd autocrat (the Viceroy of Peru). On the other hand the love of Périchole for Piquillo brings forth a genuine vein of feeling. Indeed here, Offenbach was exploiting a more serious side of his musical make-up. On this set, Berganza nicely blends the two facets of the score; so does Carreras – even though neither quite catches the French accent of words and music. They are supported by Plasson's well-tried team, and he conducts with a sure touch.

Bedřich Smetana (1824–84)

> *The Bartered Bride.* Gabriela Beňačková (Mařenka), Marie Veselá (Ludmila), Marie Mrázová (Háta), Petr Dvorský (Jeník), Miroslav Kopp (Vašek), Jaroslav Horáček (Mícha), Jindřich Jindrák (Krušina), Richard Novák (Kecal), Czech Philharmonic Ch and O/Zdeněk Košler. (Supraphon C37S-7309/11)

Smetana's operas are the musical expression of the resurgence of the Czech identity in the mid-nineteenth century. Easily the most popular of them is *Prodaná nevěsta* (literally 'Sold Bride'). Not an instant success when it appeared (1866) in its first, *opéra-comique* form, that is with spoken dialogue, it soon won favour for its vivacity and melodic profusion after the composer revised it with recitatives, instead of dialogue, and added dances – the Polka, Furiant and Dance of the Comedians – and Mařenka's last-act aria. By 1882, two years before Smetana's death, it had reached its hundredth performance in Prague, and has remained popular ever since, although it inevitably loses some of its idiomatic charm when heard, as so often, in translation. Its world of rustic comedy and its evocation of Czech folk culture demand authentic interpretation. That it receives in its most recent (1981) recording on disc, the only modern recording available on CD, and unlikely to be surpassed in the near future.

It is conducted with verve, tempered with a proper vein of sentiment, by Košler, even if the Czech Philharmonic, in a very resonant recording, sounds a shade overbearing. Dvorský, although not the equal of the great Ivo Žídek on an earlier Czech recording on LP (conducted by Jaroslav Vogel) is a likeable, confident and full-voiced Jeník, the youth who loves Mařenka. She is promised to the shy, stuttering Vašek by the egregious matchmaker Kecal. The young Beňačková, who has gone on to international fame, is here a fresh, appealing and vibrant Mařenka, wonderfully outgoing and lyrical in her aria. The experienced Novák makes a properly ripe, formidable Kecal, splendid in his pattering solo. Kopp is a more-than-adequate Vašek. The fathers and mothers of the respective lovers are all cast with experienced Czech artists. Nobody should omit getting to know this delightful piece, especially in such a satisfying performance.

Johann Strauss (1825–99)

Die Fledermaus. 1. Lucia Popp (Adele), Julia Varady (Rosalinde), Ivan Rebroff (Orlofsky), René Kollo (Alfred), Ferry Gruber (Blind), Eberhard Waechter (Eisenstein), Bernd Weikl (Falke), Benno Kusche (Frank), Bavarian State Opera Ch and O/Carlos Kleiber. (DG 415 646-2)
2. Erika Köth (Adele), Hilde Gueden (Rosalinde), Regina Resnik (Orlofsky), Giuseppe Zampieri (Alfred), Peter Klein (Blind), Waldemar Kmentt (Eisenstein), Walter Berry (Falke), Eberhard Waechter (Frank), Vienna State Opera Ch, Vienna Philharmonic O/Herbert von Karajan. (Decca 421 046-2)

Towering above Strauss's other operettas and most of its successors, this work has delighted generations of audiences since its Vienna première in 1874. At once a celebration of the Vienna waltz and a sharp satire of current Viennese society (*cf* Schnitzler), the cynicism saves the story and music from sentimentality.

Too often this work has been overlaid with an excess of self-indulgent slapstick, especially where the tiresome jailer Frosch (a speaking part) is concerned, or with too flamboyant a setting. There is a suggestion of this in the Karajan version listed above, which includes 'party pieces' by various celebrated singers then on Decca's roster. On the other hand it has tremendous *brio*, a real sense of the theatre, and above all an authentic Viennese cast. Gueden, as experienced as any, is a knowing and effervescent Rosalinde, and Köth a lively Adele. Kmentt (a tenor, rather than a baritone, as Strauss intended for the role) sings Eisenstein with aplomb; Zampieri makes fun of Italian-tenor foibles as Alfred. Berry and Waechter are at ease with their roles. The added turns include Birgit Nilsson singing 'I could have danced all night', Jussi Björling in 'Dein ist mein ganzes Herz', and Giulietta Simionato and Ettore Bastianini in a rip-roaring account of 'Anything you can do, I can do better'.

The weakness is in Regina Resnik's Orlofsky. She is too blowzy and sings her/his couplets a third down. As it happens the role is even more unsuitably cast on the Kleiber version, where it's taken by a kind of counter-tenor to disastrous effect (it should be sung by a high mezzo). But everything else here is a delight, not least Varady's spirited Rosalinde balanced by Popp's vivacious, pertly articulate Adele. Prey is a baritone Eisenstein but one who can take all the tenor notes. Kollo is a suitably fatuous Alfred, Weikl a lively Falke, Kusche an experienced Frank. But the performance's greatest asset is Kleiber's ebullient, perfectly timed conducting. As it happens he has more recently made a video/laserdisc version (also DG) with another not so distinguished cast, but – as luck has it – with the best of all Orlofskys in Brigitte Fassbaender. As a whole the production is a shade self-indulgent but authentically so.

Recommended alternative: Herbert von Karajan (EMI) – this 36-year-old mono set, carefully produced, benefits from Elisabeth Schwarzkopf's ravishing Rosalinde, Rita Streich's charming and sprightly Adele, Nicolai Gedda's classic Eisenstein and excellent support. It is a winning combination, hardly touched by the passing of the years.

Alexander Borodin (1833–87)

Prince Igor. Stefka Evstatieva (Yaroslavna), Alexandrina Milcheva (Konchakovna), Kaludi Kaludov (Vladimir), Nicola Ghiuselev (Prince Galitsky), Nicolai Ghiaurov (Khan Konchak), Sofia National Opera Ch and O/Emil Tchakarov. (Sony CD44878)

Borodin's sprawling epic was left uncompleted at his death. Various hands helped with the uncompleted orchestration, including Rimsky-Korsakov and Glazunov, and no accurate critical edition has yet appeared. Since it was the most sketchily composed, Act 3 has often been omitted in performance and recording, but its inclusion is essential to an understanding of this 'musical pageant of mediaeval Russia' (David Hamilton). Even with its inclusion many loose ends are left untied. However the fact that it is given in this version would commend it as the best available, even if it were not such a vivid and authentic-sounding performance, conducted by Tchakarov, who died recently. He lived just long enough to complete his cycle of Russian operas for Sony, carefully cast from East European singers with an understanding of the idiom. Borodin's score needs a deal of singing.

With voices of the appropriate weight and character – as here – the music takes on a truly idiomatic warmth and ardour. Igor's travails at home and abroad, the trials of his loyal wife Yaroslavna, assailed by the lecherous Prince Galitsky in her husband's absence, and the love of Igor's son Vladimir for Konchakovna, daughter of the magnanimous Tartar ruler Konchak, who has captured him and Igor, but treats them kindly, are all depicted in arias and ensembles evincing a definite colour and character to which Tchakarov and his singers generously respond. Evstatieva's warm-hearted Yaroslavna and Ghiaurov's experienced Konchak are notable, while Ghiuselev has a high old time as the rollicking Galitsky. The choruses, so important here, are superbly delivered.

Recommended alternative: Jerzy Semkow (EMI) – this version, lacking Act 3, is favoured by the important presence of Boris Christoff as both Galitsky and Khan Konchak.

Amilcare Ponchielli (1834–86)

La Gioconda: Maria Callas (Gioconda), Fiorenza Cossotto (Laura), Irene Compañeez (La Cieca), Pier Miranda Ferraro (Enzo Grimaldo), Piero Cappuccilli (Barnaba), Ivo Vinco (Alvise), Ch and O of La Scala, Milan/Antonino Votto. (EMI CDS7 49518-2)

In the United States and Italy, this piece remains part of the staple repertory; in Britain it still awaits a professional production in the post-war era. Apparently British taste is too fastidious for the overt melodrama, which some would call high-class hokum, of Ponchielli's opera to a libretto by 'Tobia Gorrio' (Arrigo Boito, Verdi's librettist, an anagrammatical disguise). It is a strong, melodious score with a succession of effective situations. These are brought to life by a taut text enhanced by the composer's ability to write arias and ensembles that really stir the listener's emotions, provided they are satisfactorily sung. Ponchielli was particularly successful at enumerating the inner feelings of his heroine, the ballad singer ironically named Gioconda, an unhappy girl, whose love for the Genoese, sea-faring nobleman Enzo Grimaldo, in seventeenth-century Venice, is thwarted by *his* love for Laura, wife of Alvise, an Inquisition supremo. The evil Barnaba, an Inquisition spy, loves Gioconda, and ruthlessly manipulates her feelings. Gioconda takes poison rather than submit to him, but not before she has forgiven Enzo and has arranged for him and Laura to escape the clutches of Alvise.

Gioconda was a role ideally fitted to Callas's gifts – she made her Italian début in it, in 1947. This, her second recording of the opera, dates from 1959 and she delivers it with complete conviction. Everything she does seems inevitable and right as she moulds text and music to portray all Gioconda's conflicting emotions, including a superb account of the final act. She once declared of her performance in this act: 'It's all there for anyone who cares to understand or wishes to know what I was about.' Gioconda's famous soliloquy 'Suicidio!', in which she determines on her course of action, is sung with appropriate fatalistic intensity. This mesmeric reading is supported by Cossotto's vibrant Laura and Cappuccilli's fierce but unsubtle Barnaba, Ferraro's stentorian but rudely effective Enzo, and Vinco as an imposing Alvise. Votto makes a few unnecessary cuts but is sensitive to the score's colour and variety.

Recommended alternatives: Bruno Bartoletti (Decca) – Montserrat Caballé is a persuasive Gioconda, more restrained than Callas, and sings with her usual distinction and subtlety of phrase. Agnes Baltsa is a vulnerable Laura, Pavarotti a predictably ardent Enzo, Sherrill Milnes a snarling, sinister Barnaba, and Nicolai Ghiaurov a powerful Alvise. Zinka Milanov's version on RCA/BMG is worth investigating should it appear on CD – she was a famous Gioconda. Rosa Ponselle's 'Suicidio' (RCA GD87810) is a classic.

Camille Saint-Saëns (1835–1921)

Samson et Dalila. Rita Gorr (Dalila), Jon Vickers (Samson), Ernest Blanc (High Priest of Dagon), Anton Diakov (Abi-mélech, Old Hebrew), René Duclos Ch, Paris Opéra O/Georges Prêtre. (EMI CDS 47895-8)

Saint-Saëns was one of the longest lived composers of his day, but he never repeated the huge success enjoyed by this work, which still sustains its place in the repertory. Surviving the shafts of Shaw, bans by the Lord Chamberlain and cries of 'oratorio' from New York pundits, it continues to please audiences whenever it is performed, not least for its suggestion of the pagan and the exotic. Martin Cooper compared the piece to Stravinsky's *Oedipus Rex* (qv) where 'the perennial and the archaic, the "modern" and the trivial are amalgamated into a convincing unity'. The composer certainly learnt much from Handel, Gluck, Berlioz, the Verdi of *Aida*, and Wagner, but from these excellent models he forged his own style and a piece in which authority, compassion, sensuality and tragedy all play their part and in which the three principals are characters of flesh and blood.

The work calls for two generous-voiced and dramatic singers in the title roles. Vickers declaims with strength, feeling and dignity of expression, although he sometimes indulges in a sentimentality that is foreign to Samson's nature. Gorr sings with rich, well-shaped tone in excellent French, but without the ultimate in voluptuousness that the part demands. Blanc is properly preening as the odious and buttoned-up High Priest. Prêtre's direction is by turns thrusting and sensuous, but his tempi, initially well chosen, are sometimes unstable. The chorus and orchestra are excellent, the recording reasonable for its day (1962).

Recommended alternatives: Daniel Barenboim (DG) – this 1978 set, based on performances at the huge arena in Orange, is admirable in all but one crucial respect. Barenboim conducts with a realisation of the work's nature. Domingo sings a noble Samson. But Elena Obraztsova is a harsh-toned, uningratiating Dalila. Colin Davis (Philips) – Agnes Baltsa is a seductive, but slightly uneven Dalila; José Carreras an impassioned, tragic Samson. Davis's evident love for the work sometimes leads him into slow speeds. The recording, made with Covent Garden forces, is the best the work has yet had.

Léo Delibes (1836–91)

Lakmé. Joan Sutherland (Lakmé), Jane Berbié (Mallika), Alain Vanzo (Gérald), Claude Calès (Frédéric), Gabriel Bacquier (Nilakantha), Monte Carlo Opera Ch and O/Richard Bonynge. (Decca 425 485-2)

Delibes's perfumed score is more than the duet made familiar by a British Airways' advertisement on television a few years ago. The hero Gérald conforms to the type presented by Puccini's Lieutenant Pinkerton, an officer who succumbs to the exotic charms of the East. It also has some resemblances to Bizet's *Pêcheurs de Perles* (qv) in that the heroine is a Brahmin priestess. Here, as in the Bizet, the priestess returns the tenor's love, but in this case is thwarted by her father Nilakantha's hatred of the British. The outcome is predictably tragic. The score is for the most part sensuous and unpretentiously lyrical in a vein typical of French music at the time of its composition (1883). It became famous not for the above-mentioned duet, but for the fiendish *coloratura* of the Bell Song, often sung on its own in the days of 78rpm records. Here it is encompassed with consummate ease by Sutherland. Elsewhere her French diction is occluded – in marked contrast to the clear enunciation of her French colleagues. Vanzo is an ideal Gérald, the rest of the singers all well suited by their parts. The 23-year-old recording wears its years lightly.

Georges Bizet (1838-1875)

Carmen. Julia Migenes (Carmen), Faith Esham (Micaëla), Placido Domingo (Don José), Ruggero Raimondi (Escamillo), French Radio Ch, French National Orchestra/Lorin Maazel. (Erato 2292-45207-2)

Although this is one of the most popular operas in the whole repertory, it has never received a definitive recording. The reasons are not hard to seek. For years it was performed in the corrupt version using recitatives composed by Ernest Guiraud after the composer's death. Since the original version, with dialogue, has been restored to favour, it has been difficult to find French singers of the right calibre to record it. Then there have been the complications created by Fritz Oeser's supposedly authentic edition of the score in the 1970s, which was found to have included passages Bizet definitely excised, for good theatrical reasons, before the première, yet conductors persist in performing these rejected sections.

By a small margin Maazel's is the recommended version, playing a reasonable text and benefiting from being the soundtrack of Rosi's film of the work in that it seems as if it were a real performance as opposed to one made in the studio. Maazel does not make the mistake of many distinguished conductors of blowing up the piece beyond its original *opéra-comique* proportions. His approach is swift and mercurial while paying due attention to the more sensuous, heady side of the score. Migenes's Carmen is at once vivid, sensual and fiery. She develops the character unerringly from the airy individuality of the first two acts through the sombre thoughts of the Card Scene to the tragic, fatalistic woman of the denouement. Vocally she exudes erotic power naturally without the exaggerations employed by so many interpreters of the role. Domingo's José has been heard in three recordings: this is probably the best of them. He may not have the good manners of French style at his command as does Gedda (see below) or some French tenors of the past, but he suggests all José's unbridled infatuation with Carmen. Raimondi is a properly preening Escamillo with the range for this awkwardly written role. Esham is an adequate Micaëla, no more.

Recommended alternatives: Claudio Abbado (DG) – this finely honed performance was also based on live performances, this time at the Edinburgh Festival in 1977, an unforgettably atmospheric staging by Piero Faggioni. Much of the feeling of that closely knit production has been carried over into the studio with Teresa Berganza as a Carmen out of a higher drawer than that aspired to by most interpreters, creating a haughty, defiant heroine rather than a particularly sensual gipsy. Domingo is again an impulsive José, Milnes a slightly too forceful Escamillo, Cotrubas an affecting Micaëla. Abbado opts for rather too many of the Oeser emendations. Sir Thomas Beecham (EMI) – this set uses the Guiraud recitatives, but it embodies the essence of Beecham's insouciant flair for French music. He concentrates on the wit and sensuousness of the score while not neglecting its more passion-ate elements. De los Angeles brings to Carmen all her gifts of innate musicality, also a lightness of touch others miss. Nicolai Gedda, a more heady and seductive José than Domingo, is a model of French style. Ernest Blanc is among the best of Escamillos, Janine Micheau an idiomatic, but slightly too mature Micaëla. Georges Prêtre (EMI) – Maria Callas cannot be ignored in any part she essays; here she depicts a magnetic, quick-to-anger, finally tragic character of unforgettable power. Gedda, again José, is only slightly less successful than in the Beecham set. Robert Massard is the best of all Escamillos, with just the timbre for the role. Andréa Guiot is a pleasing Micaëla.

> **Les Pêcheurs de Perles.** Barbara Hendricks (Leïla), John Aler (Nadir), Gino Quilico (Zurga), Jean-Philippe Courtis (Nourabad), Toulouse Capitole Ch and O/Michael Plasson. (EMI CDS7 49837-2)

This opera has gained fame from the tenor-baritone duet, one of opera's immortal melodies – 'Au fond du temple saint'. Few who hear it probably realise that it hymns the friendship of the tenor-fisherman Nadir and the baritone king of the fishermen, Zurga, who both love the fascinating but unattainable priestess Leïla.

Their old rivalry is renewed when Zurga realises that their oath of friendship has been broken by Nadir, who has discovered that Leïla returns his love.

As with *Carmen* there have always been textual difficulties with this score. Most of them are resolved on this, the most recent recording of the opera using an authentic edition. It also happens to be a finely interpreted reading of a score that has much more to offer, in terms of melodic abundance and fluency, and instrumental subtlety and beauty, than just that well-known duet. The artists here, all French-speaking and with the right style instilled in them, catch the essence of the piece. Hendricks may be a slightly cool Leïla, but she sings with the ethereal sound her role requires. Aler's high tenor is well-suited to Nadir's music, and Gino Quilico has the ideal weight and tone for Zurga. Plasson is the idiomatic conductor.

Recommended alternatives: Georges Prêtre (EMI) – this version has Ileana Cotrubas as a more affecting, sensuous Leïla than Hendricks, a stylish Nadir from Alain Vanzo (though his tenor is here not quite what it was) and a tolerable Zurga from Guillermo Sarabia. Pierre Dervaux (EMI) – worth hearing for Nicolai Gedda and Ernest Blanc, the best Nadir and the best Zurga on disc.

Modest Mussorgsky (1839–81)

Boris Godunov. Irina Arkhipova (Marina), Vladislav Piavko (Dmitri), Andrei Sokolov (Shuisky), Janis Sporgis (Simpleton), Yuri Mazurok (Rangoni), Alexander Vedernikov (Boris Godunov), Vladimir Matorin (Pimen), Artur Eizen (Varlaam), USSR TV Large Radio Ch and Symphony O/ Vladimir Fedoseyev. (Philips 412 281-2)

This opera portrays the Russian people in a series of great choruses and crowd scenes that have yet to be equalled. Set against this background is the personal tragedy of the tormented and conscience-haunted Tsar who has attained the throne through the murder of the true heir. Mussorgsky gives him a profile worthy of Shakespeare. The composer's powers of characterisation spread to the romantic pretender Grigory, masquerading as the true Tsar, Dmitri; the shifty adviser, Shuisky; the Polish prelate, Rangoni; and the ambitious Polish Princess, Marina, not forgetting the earthy Varlaam and the plaintive Simpleton. Here is a memorable panorama of Russian life. The vicissitudes of the work's genesis are a story in themselves. It was first written (in only seven scenes) in 1868–9, enlarged and refashioned in 1871–2, and performed and published in a reduced version in 1874. Then Rimsky-Korsakov 'improved' on the orchestration in an edition that was for long standard. Nowadays most conductors, even in Russia, give Mussorgsky's original version as on this recording, largely faithful to 1871–2.

This is a dedicated, idiomatic account of the work in a soul-searching, thoroughly prepared and finely conducted performance. The title role is sung with psychological insight and well-nourished tone by Vedernikov who is in the true line of great Russian basses in the part. He vividly portrays the Tsar's mental and physical collapse. Arkhipova is a regal Marina but the Dmitri is inclined to bleat. All the smaller parts are taken by artists well-versed in their music. As the set was made over a number of years there is some want of consistency, but that is not worrying enough to prevent recommendation.

Recommended alternative: André Cluytens (EMI) – Boris Christoff's imposing, larger-than-life portrayal of the Tsar, in the Rimsky-Korsakov version, is complemented by his cameos of Pimen and Varlaam. As the Tsar, Christoff uses his expressive voice and his command of nuance to present a commanding, anguished, tender and eventually tragic portrayal. The support is adequate rather than outstanding. Should Christoff's earlier recorded performance, conducted by the irreplaceable Issay Dobrowen, ever reappear on CD it would be preferable to this one. It also features the young Nicolai Gedda as an ardent Dmitri.

Pyotr Ilyich Tchaikovsky (1840–93)

Eugene Onegin. Galina Vishnevskaya (Tatyana), Larissa Avdeyeva (Olga), Valentina Petrova (Larina), Evgenya Verbitskaya (Filipievna), Sergei Lemeshev (Lensky), Evgeny

Belov (Onegin), Ivan Petrov (Gremin), Bolshoi Theatre Ch
and O/Boris Khaikin. (Legato LCD 163-2, mono)

Few operas are so immediately romantic and haunting as
Tchaikovsky's elegiac work based on Pushkin's poem of the same
name, in which the bored, seemingly heartless Onegin rejects the
ingenuous Tatyana after she has addressed him an impassioned
love letter (the famous Letter scene) only to regret his decision a
few years later when he meets her at a ball with her husband, the
elderly General Gremin. Too late he has discovered his own inner
feelings. Although Tatyana still loves him, she will not break her
marriage vows. Olga, Tatyana's younger sister, adores the poet
Lensky (who introduced Onegin to Tatyana at the home of
Larina, the girls' mother). At a local party, Olga flirts with Onegin
to the despair of the sensitive Lensky who challenges Onegin to a
duel in which Lensky, after singing a sad, fatalistic aria of plaintive
beauty, is killed. Tchaikovsky empathises with all his principals in
turn and characterises them unforgettably in music immediately
appropriate to each, set within the frame of choruses and dances,
suited to the country and city milieu in which the action is played.

It may seem perverse to choose a 35-year-old recording above
all others, but it is unique in its total response to Tchaikovsky's
score based on an idiomatic tradition that, in 1956, was still
virtually untouched at the Bolshoi. It features one young artist
(Vishnevskaya, then only 30), one veteran (Lemeshev), both
supreme in their roles, under the baton of Khaikin who knew
better than any how to shape and pace the score. Vishnevskaya's
vibrant, touching, impassioned Tatyana has never been surpassed, certainly not by her later self on an EMI set. Here her voice
captures all Tatyana's youthful ardour, all her inward, sincere
nature in a performance that leaps off the disc. Lemeshev, a most
stylish tenor, sings Lensky's music with a wide range of dynamics,
perfect articulation of the text and nicely judged tone, plangent
yet outgoing. Belov, the Onegin, though not in that class, is also
an idiomatic performer well inside his part. Petrov is a sonorous
Gremin, shaping his warm-hearted aria with poise and profile.
Chorus and orchestra perform in the best tradition of Russian
opera.

Suggested alternative: Emil Tchakarov (Sony) – This 1990 set, made with excellent Bulgarian forces (part of Sony's Russian series), is well conducted and features Nicolai Gedda as an aristocratic Lensky, recorded a little late in his career, and Yuri Mazurok as an idiomatic if inflexible Onegin. The recording is spacious and alive, with a deal of the right atmosphere inevitably missing in the Khaikin version.

> **The Queen of Spades.** Stefka Evstatieva (Lisa), Stefania Toczyska (Paulina), Penka Dilova (Countess), Wieslaw Ochman (Hermann), Ivan Konsulov (Tomsky), Yuri Mazurok (Yeletsky), Svetoslav Obretnov National Ch, Sofia Festival O/Emil Tchakarov. (Sony CD 45720)

For this, his second most popular opera, Tchaikovsky again turned to a Pushkin poem, but here the libretto by Modest Tchaikovsky, the composer's brother, alters the emphasis of the story of the cold-blooded officer seeking the secret of the three cards, uninterested in Lisa except insofar as she can gain him contact with the old Countess who possesses the required information. In the opera Hermann becomes an almost Byronic hero torn between genuine love of Lisa and his obsession with gambling. Whatever the arguments about the changes, the libretto was ideally suited to Tchaikovsky's penchant for creating the mood and passions of unhappy romances and for the kind of eccentric character represented by the Countess, whose haunting scene of reminiscence is one of the most arresting in all Russian opera. As a whole, the work – on a grander scale than *Onegin* – is filled with wonderfully evocative music, orchestrated with that command of delineating atmosphere that was the composer's forte.

In the distant past there have been several Russian recordings that matched the piece's mood and emotional power, notably that from the 1950s conducted by Melik-Pashaev with Nelepp as the most tortured and intense Hermann on disc. Excerpts from this set on Pearl CDs devoted to Russian tenors (GEMM CD 9320) are well worth finding. The recommended set, the most recent to appear, is quite the best of recent versions. Aided by a splendid choir and orchestra, Tchakarov fulfils all the many demands placed by Tchaikovsky on his interpreters in a superbly integrated recording. Ochman may not have quite enough voice for the most strenuous moments in the near-heroic role of Hermann but he does get into the soul of the man and project his anguished feelings. Evstatieva offers a deeply felt, resplendent Lisa capable of encompassing her two difficult arias. Penkova's Countess may not be as vivid as some, but is evenly sung. Mazurok sings Yeletsky's expansive aria with the firm tone and long breath it calls for. Whatever you do, don't overlook this piece of memorable music-theatre.

Antonin Dvořák (1841-1904)

Rusalka. Gabriela Beňačková (Rusalka), Drahomíra Drob-ková (Foreign Princess), Věra Soukupová (Ježibaba, a Witch), Wieslaw Ochman (Prince), Jindřich Jindrák (Game-keeper), Richard Novák (Water-Sprite), Prague Philhar-monic Ch, Czech Philharmonic O/Václav Neumann. (Supraphon 11 03641-2)

Dvořák, well-known for his orchestral and chamber works, has made headway as a composer of operas beyond his homeland (where several other of his stage works are quite frequently performed) only with this piece (1901). Rusalka, the naiad of the lake, for love of a prince persuades a witch to change her into human form even though this means she will be mute. The Prince returns her love, but comes to realise that he wants human passion. He is lured away from Rusalka by a Foreign Princess. The Prince's yearning for Rusalka leads him to seek her in the lake. She kisses him and he dies, but she lives for ever to lure other humans to their doom. Dvořák clothes the libretto in lyrical beauty and haunting poetry in a score suffused with a sense of water. Rusalka's aria, known in English as 'O silver moon', has gained a popularity on its own account.

This 1983 recording is an authentic representation of the work and its peculiarly Czech character. Beňačková's soaring and impassioned singing of the title role is the set's main attraction and she sings the Moon song as to the manner born. Ochman is an ardent and articulate prince, Novák an appropriately gruff though benign Water-Sprite. The veteran Soukupová is a louring, forceful Witch. Nobody is more adept at conducting Dvořák's music today than Neumann who makes the most of the score's lyrical flights and luminous scoring. The dynamic range of the recording adds to the set's appreciable worth.

Jules Massenet (1842–1912)

Manon. Victoria de los Angeles (Manon), Henri Legay (Des Grieux), René Hérent (Guillot), Michel Dens (Lescaut), Jean Vieuille (de Brétigny), Jean Borthayre (Comte des Grieux), Ch and O of the Opéra-Comique, Paris/Pierre Monteux. (EMI CMS7 63549-2 (mono))

Massenet's famous setting of the Abbé Prévost's novel, more faithful to the original than is Puccini's setting (qv) of the same book, concentrates on different episodes in the story. Massenet perfectly adumbrates the spoilt, seductive, fickle, charming nature of the heroine in a number of solos and duets with her lover, the obsessed Chevalier Des Grieux, who is delineated with similar perception. Massenet's singular, individual style of writing calls for singers with good French able to make the most of the text who will also follow the composer's scrupulous markings where dynamics and expression are concerned. Such combined attributes have been hard to come by in a generation of all-purpose, international singers so that it is hardly surprising that EMI's 1955 set still holds sway. It was in its day a remarkably faithful mono recording and that high quality has been further enhanced in its CD transfer.

Monteux made all too few complete recordings of opera. Here he was in his element conducting the forces of the Opéra-Comique then still steeped in a tradition of giving the piece which by then stretched to more than two thousand performances in its home, the Salle Favart. The smaller parts are taken by singers who had learnt their trade from some of the earliest interpreters of the opera. Vieuille and Hérent were by 1955 veterans, Borthayre and Dens at the peak of their careers. All four represent a style now virtually lost. De los Angeles made the title role very much her own. She is at once as enchanting as Des Grieux describes her at their first meeting and later frivolous and, at her death, most moving. The Spanish soprano's timbre, warm yet light, is ideal for her part, which she delivers with exquisite phrasing and clear, pointed diction. She is worthily partnered by Legay, whose eager, youthful and when needed impassioned tenor is only slightly too light for the more heroic parts of his role. The voices of heroine and hero blend beautifully. Altogether this is a set that has rightly stood the test of time, one of the classics among recorded opera, even though one or two minor cuts are made.

Recommended alternatives: Michel Plasson (EMI) – this is the best of modern versions with Ileana Cotrubas giving a supple, affecting account of the title role and Alfredo Kraus as a well-seasoned Des Grieux. One would have liked them, however, to have recorded their parts a few years earlier when both were in their prime. The work is given complete. Élie Cohen (EPM Classical Collector/Conifer) – this version dates from as long ago as 1932. It embodies, even more truthfully than the Monteux set, the original way of performing the work at the Opéra-Comique with Germaine Féraldy as an adorable heroine and Joseph Rogatchewsky (Russian by birth, French by adoption) as a near-ideal Des Grieux, plangent in tone, ardent in manner, creating a very present picture of the obsessed Des Grieux.

Werther. Ninon Vallin (Charlotte), Germaine Féraldy (Sophie), Georges Thill (Werther), Emile Rocque (Albert), Armand Narçon (Bailli), Ch and O of the Opéra-Comique, Paris/Élie Cohen. (EMI CHS7 63195-2, mono)

This work shows Massenet even more adept than in the earlier *Manon* at relating words to music, a conversational style that blossoms into *arioso* or even full-blown aria. Here this style is at the service of a setting of Goethe's romantic novel with the fatalistic, love-lorn, attitudinizing Werther as its hero and the still-waters-run-deep Charlotte as the unattainable object of his thwarted desires: when they fall in love she is already promised to the stiff but safe Albert. Massenet perfectly captures the emotional feelings of his principals without ever resorting to rhetorical gesture. He may have learnt something new about orchestration, by the time he wrote this work, through hearing Wagner, but the lesson is rightly subsumed in his own, very French manner. That manner, as with *Manon*, is an inward, reflective enunciation of the principals' feelings.

It is still best represented by the famous 1931 performance listed above in which Ninon Vallin's warm tone, distinctive style, poised, restrained yet vibrant with emotion, matches Charlotte's role to perfection. It would be hard to imagine the part being better interpreted, and indeed none of her successors has quite emulated her success in it. Opposite her is Thill as unquestionably the most idiomatic protagonist on disc, at once impassioned but never exaggerated in his projection of Werther's predicament, and singing with an ease and balance that puts all other interpreters in the shade. One of the great tenors of the century, Thill was properly fêted in France during the 1920s and '30s. Both his and Vallin's art can be heard on separate EMI CDs comprising examples of their respective repertories, but neither did anything better than this *Werther*. Féraldy makes a nice foil to Vallin's Charlotte – effervescent, bright in a very French way. The Albert and Bailli (Charlotte's father) are both excellent. Cohen balances elegance and passion in just the right measure.

Recommended alternative: Michel Plasson (EMI) – most convincing of modern versions with Alfredo Kraus as a stylish Werther and Tatiana Troyanos as an impassioned Charlotte.

Other Massenet:
Massenet's large output, some of it indifferent in quality, includes several pieces that deserve to be heard more often.

Thaïs used to be popular, particularly in France, and it deserves more attention today. It tells of the young monk Athanaël's move from religious fanaticism, in fourth-century Alexandria, to obsessive love for the courtesan Thaïs, while she makes the journey from sensual to religious love. Massenet grasped the irony and indeed the sadness of this situation as related in Anatole France's novella and converted it unerringly into musical terms. The setting is notable for Massenet's unique ability to write in a kind of conversational style that moves easily and imperceptibly into aria or *arioso*, the music controlled by the composer's gift for setting speech precisely and pointedly. (His copious and strict marks of dynamic and expression are famous.) The only recording available at present (Chant du Monde) derives from a French radio broadcast of 1959. It features the charming Thaïs of Andrée Esposito and the classic Athanaël of Robert Massard, one of the leading French baritones of his generation. The conductor is the veteran Albert Wolff.

Thaïs (1894) followed *Manon* (1884) and *Werther* (1892) and showed an even greater refinement of means. The process was carried still further in two of Massenet's late works, both written for the Monte Carlo Opéra, where he was much admired. *Le Jongleur de Notre Dame* is a short, mesmeric piece in which the 'discreet and semi-religious eroticism' (as composer Vincent D'Indy graphically put it) for which Massenet was renowned finds further expression in the story of the tumbler who devotes himself to the Virgin at Cluny abbey in fourteenth-century France. A work of reticent charm, it has the recording it deserves (Chant du Monde) under the musical direction of Pierre Dervaux, a French radio broadcast of 1973 with Alain Vanzo as the tumbler Jean and Massard splendid as the tetchy Brother Boniface.

Massenet's last success was *Don Quichotte* in which the errant knight of the title and his faithful Sancho Panza are lovingly depicted. This is another charming score, which receives a rewarding performance on a Decca recording with Nicolai Ghiaurov in the title role, most eloquent in Quichotte's famous death scene where he has a vision of his beloved Dulcinée, and Gabriel Bacquier as a characterful Sancho. Régine Crespin fills the colourful music for Dulcinée with the right flirtatious profile.

Arrigo Boito (1842–1918)

Mefistofele. Mirella Freni (Margherita), Montserrat Caballé (Elena), Luciano Pavarotti (Faust), Nicolai Ghiaurov (Mefistofele), Trinity Boys' Ch, National Philharmonic O/Oliviero De Fabritiis. (Decca 410 175-2)

Boito is a curious figure in the history of opera. He was a true intellectual; indeed his musical gifts were not always equal to his intelligence. He has become best known as the librettist of Verdi's two late masterpieces, *Otello* and *Falstaff*. However, his Faust opera, *Mefistofele*, has continued to hold the stage, especially in

Italy. It was produced when he was only sixteen. For the remaining fifty years of his life he laboured on the score of his only other opera *Nerone* (available on a Hungaroton recording), eventually staged after his death at La Scala. Although an uneven work, *Mefistofele* has several arresting passages, most notably the Prologue in heaven and Margherita's famous lament 'L'altra notte', intriguingly recorded by Muzio (see recital discs) and Callas.

This recording gives the work its due. The veteran de Fabritiis conducts it with authority. Pavarotti sings with liquid, heady tone as Faust, and Freni is a touching Margherita. It is luxury casting indeed to have Caballé as Elena (Helen of Troy) for her single appearance. But the opera stands or falls by the bass impersonating Mefistofele. Ghiaurov is suitably imposing – although Samuel Ramey on the rival Sony recording, with Domingo as Faust, is as imposing. That set is lamed by Eva Marton's coarse singing of both Margherita and Elena.

Arthur Sullivan (1842–1900)

HMS Pinafore. Elizabeth Ritchie (Josephine), Linda Ormiston (Buttercup), Christopher Gillett (Ralph Rackstraw), Nickolas Grace (Sir Joseph Porter), Gordon Sandison (Captain Corcoran), Thomas Lawlor (Dick Deadeye), Ch and O of New Sadler's Wells Opera/Simon Phipps. (TER CDTER2 1150)

This satire on the navy, one of the earliest and best of G&S successes, here receives a lively performance from the now-defunct New Sadler's Wells Opera company, which performed it on stage with such gusto. The cast is mainly comprised of established opera artists who sing with flair and gusto. They are supplemented by Grace's amusing Sir Joseph. The whole thing, while traditional in the best sense, is released from hidebound D'Oyly Carte ways.

Patience. Mary Sansom (Patience), Gillian Knight (Jane), John Reed (Bunthorne), Kenneth Sandford (Grosvenor),

Donald Adams (Colonel Calverley), D'Oyly Carte Opera Ch, New Symphony O/Isidore Godfrey. (Decca 425 193-2)

This delightful piece satirizes at once the *fin du siècle* movement among artists and the foibles of the military. This D'Oyly Carte performance, including some well-known regulars of the 1960s and '70s, is notable for including some of Gilbert's wittiest dialogue.

Iolanthe. Mary Sansom (Phyllis), Yvonne Newman (Iolanthe), Gillian Knight (Queen of the Fairies), Alan Styler (Strephon), John Reed (Lord Chancellor), Kenneth Sandford (Private Willis), D'Oyly Carte Opera Ch, New Symphony O/Isidore Godfrey. (Decca 414 145-2)

Here the target is the House of the Lords when it comes into contact with the world of fairies. Sullivan introduces for the first time a vein of sentiment into the Savoy operas. This version, with dialogue, is a fair representation of the piece.

The Mikado. Valerie Masterson (Yum-Yum), Lyndsie Holland (Katisha), Colin Wright (Nanki-Poo), Kenneth Sandford (Pooh-Bah), John Reed (Ko-Ko), John Ayldon (Mikado), D'Oyly Carte Opera Ch, Royal Philharmonic O/Royston Nash. (Decca 417 296-2)

This set derives from one of the last generations of the D'Oyly Carte company, which includes the lovely Yum-Yum of Valerie Masterson, and several well-tried regulars, but dialogue is excluded. The piece is more a satire of class and social manners than of things Japanese, as Jonathan Miller realised in his superb, updated ENO staging, alas not yet recorded.

Ruddigore. Marilyn Hill Smith (Rose Maybud), Linda Ormiston (Mad Margaret), Joan Davies (Dame Hannah), David Hillman (Richard Dauntless), Harold Innocent (Sir Despard Murgatroyd), Thomas Lawlor (Sir Roderick Murgatroyd), John Ayldon (Old Adam), Ch and O of New Sadler's Wells Opera/Simon Phipps. (TER 21128)

Another performance taken from New Sadler's Wells's excellent revivals of the 1980s. The score is one of Sullivan's best and Gilbert's dialogue, though somewhat less sharp-edged than in the past, still has its moments. The plot is suitably bizarre, concerned with inheritance, curses and ghosts.

> *The Yeomen of the Guard.* Elizabeth Harwood (Elsie Maynard), Ann Hood (Phoebe), Gillian Knight (Dame Carruthers), Philip Potter (Colonel Fairfax), John Reed (Jack Point), Kenneth Sandford (Wilfred Shadbolt), Donald Adams (Sergeant Meryll), Anthony Raffell (Sir Richard Cholmondeley), D'Oyly Carte Opera Ch, Royal Philharmonic O/Malcolm Sargent. (Decca SKL 4624-5)

This is the only G&S score to end tragically; it is also the most serious and extended of the Savoy Operas. Under Sargent's sympathetic baton it receives a well-tended performance, with a cast headed by the late-lamented Elizabeth Harwood and Reed, at his best as Jack Point. It is partnered with the early and uproarious *Trial by Jury* featuring Thomas Round's caddish defendant and Reed's tetchy Judge.

> *The Gondoliers.* Mary Sansom (Gianetta), Jennifer Toye (Casilda), Gillian Knight (The Duchess of Plaza-Toro), Jeffrey Skitch (Luiz), Thomas Round (Marco Palmieri), Alan Styler (Giuseppe Palmieri), John Reed (The Duke of Plaza-Toro), D'Oyly Carte Opera Ch, New Symphony O/Isidore Godfrey. (Decca 425 177-2)

Although this is a mellifluous, well-crafted score, the piece lacks the wit and sharp-edged satire of its predecessors: the partnership is beginning to lose its energy. This set (with dialogue), showing the latter-day D'Oyly Carte company at its best, does well by the piece.

Recommended alternatives: Arabesque and Pearl have reissued some of the early HMV recordings from the 1920s and '30s featuring such stalwarts as Sir Henry Lytton, Bertha Lewis, Derek Oldham and George Baker. These are historic documents of importance, chronicling a way of performing G&S now extinct. The recordings still sound well.

Gabriel Fauré (1845–1924)

Pénélope. Jessye Norman (Pénélope), Colette Alliot-Lugaz (Alkandre), Jocelyne Taillon (Euryclée), Alain Vanzo (Ulisse), Philippe Huttenlocher (Eurymaque), José van Dam (Eumée), Jean Laforge Ch, Monte Carlo Philharmonic O/Charles Dutoit. (Erato 2292-45405)

Fauré's *drame-lyrique*, based on the classical story of Pénélope's constancy, attempted – with success, be it said – to express 'human feelings in, if possible, more than human accents'. The libretto, by René Fauchois, allowed the composer to develop his peculiarly individual manner of writing a music-drama, influenced – inevitably – by Wagner but never subsuming his own personality to that of Bayreuth's wizard. His solution, as Nectoux (Fauré's biographer) states, 'amounts to a synthesis of forms, ranging from pure recitative to aria and marks a singular return to the beginnings of opera with Caccini and Monteverdi'. The title role is particularly eloquent. It is movingly sung by Norman on this recommendable set. (Although another, not yet on CD, with Crespin as Pénélope, is still better.) Dutoit is the sympathetic conductor and the supporting French singers all idiomatic in accent. This is a work that will repay the adventurous listener wanting to hear a fine piece off the beaten track.

Engelbert Humperdinck (1854–1921)

Hänsel und Gretel. Barbara Bonney (Gretel), Barbara Hendricks (Sandman), Eva Lind (Dew Fairy), Anne Sofie von Otter (Hänsel), Hanna Schwarz (Mother), Marjana Lipovšek (Witch), Andreas Schmidt (Father), Tölz Boys' Choir, Bavarian Radio Symphony O/Jeffrey Tate. (EMI CDS7 54022-2)

Humperdinck's fairy tale is a delight for children of all ages. Here Wagnerian methods are at the service of a pleasing fantasy. The composer deftly combines simple, folk-like melody, voices light enough to suggest the children who get lost in a wood seeking strawberries and are inveigled into the Witch's snares, and a Wagnerian orchestration apt for portraying an elaborate Dream sequence and the Witch's Ride. The piece has held its popularity now for almost a hundred years and rightly shows no sign of losing its ability to captivate an audience.

It has fared well on disc. This, its most recent recording just about matches the achievement of the classic mono version conducted by Karajan (see below) and of course benefits from excellent modern sound. Tate (who acknowledges his debt to Karajan's set) proves a sympathetic and rewarding interpreter of the piece, making the most of its many instrumental felicities and of its dreamy and supernatural elements. Bonney's fresh, girlish tone and outgoing manner is ideal for Gretel's music and von Otter's firm, vibrant, boyish tone for Hänsel. Lipovšek brings the right, exulting, preening character to the Witch's part without resorting to the caricature employed by some of her predecessors. Schmidt makes a bluff, sympathetic Father, Schwarz a properly concerned Mother. The Tölz Boys' Choir provides the ideal sound for the children saved from the Witch's clutches. The Bavarian Radio Symphony Orchestra plays with authentic brio revelling in the score's many colours.

Recommended alternatives: Herbert von Karajan (EMI) – this thirty-eight-year-old recording still holds its own against newcomers. Karajan and the vintage Philharmonia Orchestra play splendidly, Elisabeth Grümmer is an eager, exuberant Hänsel, and Elisabeth Schwarzkopf a charming but too knowing Gretel. Sir John Pritchard (CBS/Sony) – this is a loving, beautifully recorded set with Ileana Cotrubas and Frederica von Stade as delightful children, Christa Ludwig having a high old time as the Witch.

Konigskinder, Humperdinck's later, more complex fairytale opera, will repay study, especially on its excellent EMI recording, featuring Helen Donath and Adolf Dallapozza as hero and heroine.

Leoš Janáček (1854–1928)

Jenůfa. Elisabeth Söderström (Jenůfa), Lucia Popp (Karolka), Eva Randová (Kostelnička), Wieslaw Ochman (Laca), Petr Dvorský (Števa), Vienna State Opera Ch, Vienna Philharmonic O/Sir Charles Mackerras. (Decca 414 483-2)

It was the Prague production of this opera in 1916 that brought fame to Janáček. Very soon the highly original work was given quite widely in Central Europe, but it wasn't until the 1950s, when Rafael Kubelik and then Mackerras began to introduce his operas to Britain, that the composer became known in this country and the USA. Since then almost all of his operas have gained currency, although only two or three are at all regularly performed. *Jenůfa* is closest to the supposed mainstream of opera, and so remains the most often performed. It displays all his well-known traits in an early stage of their development: his expansive humanity, his love of natural sounds, the conversational ease of his declamation, all expressed in intense, heartfelt music, often of surpassing beauty. There is a poignancy, a lyrical grace and spontaneity in Janáček's writing that is unique. He felt that landscapes and people revealed their souls in 'the tracks of sounds that pass our way'.

Jenůfa tells of the love of the eponymous heroine for the unworthy Števa, by whom she has a son during the course of the opera, and for his step-brother Laca who truly loves Jenůfa. However the opera is driven by the Kostelnička, the Sextoness, daughter-in-law of Grandmother Buryia, grandmother to Števa and Laca. All ends happily, as Laca frees Jenůfa from her misery, but not before the Kostelnička has murdered Jenůfa's son, tormented by the disgrace to the family of the baby's illegitimacy. In this recording Mackerras and his singers peer into the heart of the principals in sympathy with the composer. Randová gives a performance of frightening intensity as the dictatorial Kostelnička, Söderström brings all her gifts for impersonating downtrodden heroines to the part of Jenůfa. Both tenors are ideal in their roles. In support are many stalwarts of Czech opera. The recording is superb.

Káťa Kabanová. Elisabeth Söderström (Káťa), Libuše Marová (Varvara), Naděžda Kniplová (Kabanicha), Petr Dvorský (Boris), Vladimir Krejčík (Tichon), Dalibor Jedlička (Dikoy), Vienna State Opera Ch, Vienna Philharmonic O/Sir Charles Mackerras. (Decca 421 852-2)

This was the first opera to make its way in Britain, thanks to a famous production, conducted by Kubelik, at Sadler's Wells. It has since been staged faithfully all over the country. It was first given at Brno, where Janáček lived and was best known, in 1921. It tells of sensitive, impulsive Káťa, married to the weak merchant Tichon, but in love with Boris, a cultivated, romantic youth from Moscow. In the end, left alone by Boris and tormented by guilt, she throws herself into the Volga. Again there is a dominating older woman, the cold, respectable Kabanicha, mother of Tichon. Janáček catches to perfection the claustrophobic atmosphere in which Káťa's illicit passion develops. Altogether the characterisation, as in all Janáček's scores, closely follows the conflicting, changing emotions of the principals.

This 1976 recording was the first of the highly successful Janáček sets made by Decca. Mackerras is wholly in sympathy with the ethos of the piece, as is his devoted cast, headed by Söderström's moving Káťa and the keenly lyrical Boris of the young Dvorský. The veteran Kniplová is a virulent Kabanicha. The playing of the VPO is superb – as is the recording.

The Cunning Little Vixen. Lucia Popp (Vixen), Eva Randová (Fox), Dalibor Jedlička (Forester), Bratislava Children's Ch, Vienna State Opera Ch, Vienna Philharmonic O/Sir Charles Mackerras. (Decca 417 129-2)

A set of newspaper drawings was the inspiration for this extraordinarily inspired score, first given in Brno in 1924, in which the sounds of the forest and of the natural world easily elide with that of the human environment. While there is plenty of anthropomorphic charm in the score, the composer quite avoids whimsy and any twee feeling, although some producers have succumbed to the temptation of playing the piece that way. The frisky Vixen herself shows feminist leanings before that was the norm, while she also becomes a sex symbol for both animals and humans. No wonder she comes to a sticky end. The wonder of the orchestration is ideally projected in this vital recording, made in 1982. Popp makes a sparky, verbally alert Vixen, and receives splendid support from an experienced Czech cast. This inexhaustibly fascinating work will give many hours of delight. What an amazing achievement it remains from a seventy-year-old composer. The alternative EMI set, conducted by Simon Rattle, is worthwhile for those wanting to hear the work in English.

Giacomo Puccini (1858–1924)

Manon Lescaut. Maria Callas (Manon Lescaut), Giuseppe di Stefano (Des Grieux), Giulio Fioravanti (Lescaut), Franco Calabrese (Geronte), Ch and O of La Scala, Milan/Tullio Serafin. (EMI CDS7 47393-8 (mono))

Puccini's first success isn't among his most cogently conceived scores, but it is wonderfully spontaneous and immediate in its appeal. Puccini captured the feeling of the ardent, sensual love between Manon and the infatuated Des Grieux in an entirely different way from Massenet (qv), choosing different episodes from Abbé Prévost's novel. Puccini wrote to his publisher: 'Manon is a heroine I believe in – she cannot fail to win the hearts of the public.' And so it proved. This is the first of his operas where his melody, profuse and memorable, takes on its own, individual accent.

It calls for the utmost fervour from its two principals; that Callas and di Stefano amply supply. Callas catches admirably the spoilt, capricious side of Manon's nature, which is her final undoing as she tries to round up all the goodies her elderly admirer, Geronte, has given her rather than escaping while she can with her true love, Chevalier Des Grieux. Callas is at once a vulnerable, seductive, teasing and in the end – exiled in Louisiana and dying – tragic figure. Hers is a fully rounded portrait of a lovable creature, derived as much from Prévost's original story as from Puccini, and, as ever, Callas makes any role she is undertaking wholly her own. Di Stefano, always at his best when most ardent, catches the hectic, subjective character of Des Grieux's love for Manon. His singing nicely combines delicacy and full-throated attack. The all-Italian support is excellent, as is Serafin's authoritative conducting.

Recommended alternative: Giuseppe Sinopoli (DG) – a very acceptable modern performance with Mirella Freni as an appealing, warm Manon, Placido Domingo as a passionate Des Grieux. Sinopoli is liable to eccentricities of tempo, but his reading is as finely detailed as the recording itself.

La Bohème. Renata Tebaldi (Mimì), Gianna d'Angelo (Musetta), Carlo Bergonzi (Rodolfo), Ettore Bastianini (Marcello), Renato Cesari (Schaunard), Cesare Siepi (Colline), Santa Cecilia Academy Ch and O/Tullio Serafin. (Decca 425 534-2)

Puccini's first masterpiece is notable for its taut, keenly fashioned structure, its abundance of melody, and its economy of characterisation. Over-riding all these is its immediate appeal to the emotions: Mimì's genuine love for her Rodolfo rudely cut short by tuberculosis, lovingly expressed by Puccini, and the youthful exuberance of the four Bohemians, have kept it in the forefront of the public's concept of what opera should be ever since its creation. Not surprisingly there have been a number of notable recordings, the most prized being the classic set conducted by Beecham (see below), but the roughly contemporaneous version conducted by Serafin is a more idiomatic, more Italianate and warmer account of the score. Its merits comprise the essence of Puccini performance.

Mimì was one of Tebaldi's best-loved creations. Her reading may not be as closely characterised as some, but it is as heartfelt and generously sung as any, and she has the soaring, *spinto* tone to fulfil all Puccini's demands on his beloved heroine. She is partnered by Bergonzi in lyrical and appealing form, singing with attractive brio and just the right weight of voice. The other Bohemians are all well cast, with Siepi particularly notable as the philosopher Colline. Gianna d'Angelo is a sprightly, characterful Musetta. The recording is spacious and atmospheric.

Recommended alternatives: Beecham (EMI) – this elegantly turned set is distinguished by the touching, frail Mimì of Victoria de los Angeles and the classic Rodolfo of Jussi Björling. Antonino Votto (EMI) – Callas is Mimi here, as ever creating an individual character by the genius of her art and supported by outstanding performances from Giuseppe di Stefano as Rodolfo, Anna Moffo as Musetta and Rolando Panerai as Marcello. Herbert von Karajan (Decca) – a sumptuous, modern recording, a shade overblown for the piece, featuring Mirella Freni's noted Mimi and Pavarotti's glorious Rodolfo. All these versions are worthy representatives of a work that can enjoy many different interpretations. Indeed it is an opera that should be heard in various readings.

Tosca. Maria Callas (Tosca), Giuseppe di Stefano (Cavaradossi), Tito Gobbi (Scarpia), Ch and O of La Scala, Milan/ Victor De Sabata. (EMI CDS7 47175-8 (mono))

'Shabby little shocker' was one musicologist's notorious verdict on Puccini's melodrama based on a play by Sardou, but it hasn't interrupted the long march of the opera's success with the public. A work so unerringly crafted to capture an audience's emotions is not to be despised; even in an indifferent performance it never fails to hit the mark. When it is conducted and sung with the truthfulness and conviction shown in this classic 1953 recording, it sounds a great work. De Sabata, who made all too few recordings, projects the piece's strong emotions with emotional force. From the arresting power of the opening chords one knows this is to be a gripping interpretation – and so it proves.

In one of her earliest successes on disc, Callas fills all the appreciable demands Puccini places on his soprano. She projects Tosca's flirtatious, teasing, jealous character in Act 1, her anguish and courage in Act 2, her tender love in Act 3 when she thinks there is going to be a happy end for her and her Cavaradossi. Her clear, pointed diction, evocative, resinous tone, above all her complete involvement in the role bring the most out of Puccini's writing. Her interpretation is matched by that of the youthful di Stefano at his most fervent and impassioned. Tito Gobbi, finding in Scarpia's role all sorts of subtleties that elude other interpreters, creates a rounded portrait of the aristocratic, cynical, sneering satyr. With the mono recording still sounding well enough, this is an unbeatable performance. Callas's later recording (EMI), also with Gobbi, is less of a success: both artists have deteriorated vocally.

Recommended alternative: Herbert von Karajan (Decca) – this thirty-year-old version has stood the test of time, with an atmospheric, well-balanced recording. Leontyne Price, in lovely voice, offers an impassioned Tosca, di Stefano (a shade past his best) remains a notable Cavaradossi. Giuseppe Taddei is the baritone who comes closest to matching Gobbi's nuances as Scarpia, and his suave, mellifluous tone makes his unwanted advances to Tosca that much more insinuating.

Madama Butterfly. 1. Renata Scotto (Butterfly), Anna di Stasio (Suzuki), Carlo Bergonzi (Pinkerton), Rolando Panerai (Sharpless), Ch and O of Rome Opera/Sir John Barbirolli. (EMI CMS7 69654-2)
2. Maria Callas (Butterfly), Lucia Danieli (Suzuki), Nicolai Gedda (Pinkerton), Mario Borriello (Sharpless), Ch and O of La Scala, Milan/Herbert von Karajan. (EMI CDS7 47959-8, mono)
3. Victoria de los Angeles (Butterfly), Miriam Pirazzini (Suzuki), Jussi Björling (Pinkerton), Mario Sereni (Sharpless), Ch and O of Rome Opera/Gabriele Santini. (EMI CMS7 63634-2)

For once it is impossible to choose among rival versions. Each of these three EMI sets presents, in differing ways, an absorbing interpretation of the central part. For an all-round, intelligent, Italianate reading, Scotto is unbeatable. She catches all the role's pathos, inner meaning and Puccinian *morbidezza*, inspired by Barbirolli in the better of his two complete-opera sets, urging on his excellent Rome forces to great things. His direction is direct, affectionate and heartwarming. Bergonzi is as stylish and ardent a Pinkerton as one could wish to hear and Panerai's vibrant singing and concerned portrayal of Sharpless is the best on disc.

Callas's version is yet another of her singular and totally individual portrayals, deeply moving in Butterfly's Act 2 delusion, tragic when her hopes are proved false in Act 3. There are passages here that etch themselves indelibly into the memory like no other. Gedda is an airy Pinkerton, singing the music in a scrupulous manner unequalled by his rivals. Karajan's intense reading is another advantage of this set. Victoria de los Angeles offers another convincing way of interpreting Butterfly's character. Here sweet tone and delicate utterance prevail, combined with some marvellously sincere passages of singing – as her 'Che tua madre'. Only occasionally are we aware that hers isn't quite a Butterfly voice. Björling offers his usual virtues as an almost too stylish Pinkerton. Sereni is a properly paternal Sharpless, Pirazzini the most concerned of Suzukis.

Suggested alternative: Karajan (Decca) – this is the best of reasonably recent versions. The singing, with Mirella Freni and Pavarotti in the main roles, is suitably convincing, and the Vienna Philharmonic play superbly for Karajan. The results are splendid if just a shade overdone. Christa Ludwig is a telling Suzuki.

La Fanciulla del West. Carol Neblett (Minnie), Placido Domingo (Dick Johnson), Sherrill Milnes (Jack Rance), Robert Lloyd (Ashby), Gwynne Howell (Jake Wallace), Ch and O of Royal Opera House, Covent Garden/Zubin Mehta. (DG 419 640-2)

Minnie, the saloon-bar owner, plays mother to a whole community of gold diggers. She is loved by the bandit Ramerrez, calling himself Dick Johnson, and by the sheriff, Jack Rance, who is after Ramerrez's blood. Minnie loves Johnson and saves him from the Sherriff's clutches in a melodramatic scene. The score, full of atmospheric touches, is as seamlessly composed as any of Puccini's earlier successes, but has never quite caught the public's imagination in the same way. It was first given at the Metropolitan, New York, with a cast consisting of Emmy Destinn, Caruso and Pasquale Amato. Although they never recorded a note from the opera, they must have been an unbeatable trio. The singers here are all splendid in the roles. Two of them took part in a late '70s staging of the work at Covent Garden under the same conductor and with the same cast of British singers in the minor parts, so the performance really takes fire as if it were a live performance.

The American soprano Carol Neblett's voice and appearance

were ideal for the role, and here by voice alone she conveys all Minnie's carefree, tough attitude in Act 1, and then in Act 2 her burgeoning love for Johnson. He is taken robustly and with a deal of nervous energy by Domingo in one of his best parts. Milnes, not in the London performances, is also well cast as the rough, tough Rance and sings with splendid aplomb. Mehta, well served by his Covent Garden forces, conducts with real panache.

Il Trittico: (i) *Il tabarro*; (ii) *Suor Angelica*; (iii) *Gianni Schicchi*.
(i) Renata Scotto (Giorgetta), Placido Domingo (Luigi), Ingvar Wixell (Michele).
(ii) Renata Scotto (Suor Angelica), Ileana Cotrubas (Suor Genovieffa), Marilyn Horne (La Principessa), Patricia Payne (Abbess).
(iii) Ileana Cotrubas (Lauretta), Placido Domingo (Rinuccio), Tito Gobbi (Gianni Schicchi), New Philharmonia Ch, New Philharmonia O, LSO (for (iii) only)/Lorin Maazel. (CBS/Sony CD79312)

Il Trittico contrasts in one evening a lurid thriller, a sentimental tragedy and a rip-roaring, cynical comedy. They make an unusual unity given together, as they show Puccini's advances, by 1918, in terms of style and harmony, but even Puccini came to feel that, at about an hour each, they make a long evening in the theatre. Each works well enough on its own or paired, as sometimes happens, with a piece by another composer. *Gianni Schicchi* is undoubtedly the most popular. The reason isn't hard to find as it offers a gift of a part for an experienced baritone with a leaning towards comedy.

The most successful recordings (not yet on CD) are probably those made in the 1950s in which Gobbi sang Michele in *Il tabarro* and Schicchi. Victoria de los Angeles was a warm and moving Angelica. When Maazel came to record the three operas in the 1970s Gobbi repeated his finely detailed, tonally varied Schicchi, a wonderful example of acting with the voice. The Maazel 'cycle' is on the whole a very reasonable representation of the three operas. Scotto nicely varies her voice and manner between the voluptuous, fiery Giorgetta and the pure, sad Angelica, the girl who has taken the veil to expiate the scandal of being an unmarried mother. When her aunt, the Princess, comes to tell her that she must remain in the convent and that her child is dead,

Angelica decides on suicide. Scotto conveys Angelica's desperate predicament with her well-known ability to colour words and tone. Horne is superb as La Principessa, Cotrubas touching as the young sister Genovieffa. In *Il tabarro*, Domingo is properly ardent as Giorgetta's young, illicit lover Luigi, and Wixell magnificently fierce as her avenging husband, Luigi.

Schicchi, who masquerades as the dying Donato to rob Donato's grasping relations of their inheritance, bequeathing it to himself instead, is a lovable old rogue as depicted in the only score where Puccini really deployed and extended his gift for witty comedy. As already suggested, Gobbi makes the most of the title role. Cotrubas is an appealing Lauretta, singing the famous 'O mio babbino caro' with appropriate charm. Domingo is a forthright Rinuccio.

Turandot. Birgit Nilsson (Turandot), Renata Scotto (Liù), Franco Corelli (Calaf), Bonaldo Giaiotti (Timur), Ch and O of Rome Opera/Francesco Molinari-Pradelli. (EMI CMS7 69327)

Puccini's last, uncompleted opera tells the fairy-tale story of the cruel, chaste eastern Princess of the title. She slays all pretenders to her hand who cannot solve her three riddles. At last an unknown prince, in fact Calaf, son of the exiled King of Tartary, answers the riddle successfully. He says, magnanimously, that he will still agree to die if she can discover his name by dawn. In desperation Turandot has Liù, a slave girl in love with the Prince tortured to disclose his name. She refuses, then stabs herself. At this point Puccini's contribution ends. His colleague, Alfano, completed the opera, which meant writing – from the composer's sketches – the happy end, in which the ice princess finally capitulates to Calaf's ardent advances. Alfano's effort is worthy enough – but the music is in no way the equal of Puccini's. It is possible that Puccini was subconsciously unwilling or unable to complete the opera.

Turandot is one of the ultimate challenges for a dramatic soprano. Few in any generation are capable of fulfilling its inordinate demands (even though the part isn't long). In recent times Nilsson has been far and away its best equipped interpreter. Here, in the second and better of her two recorded performances, she sings with unflagging power and unfailingly steady and controlled tone while also managing to inject the role with just the right combination of chilly isolation and womanly vulnerability. Her achievement is matched by Corelli's handsome-voiced Calaf; he sings the now-famous 'Nessun dorma' with trumpet-like tone and fervent energy. Scotto, in the lyrical part of Liù, last of Puccini's put-upon heroines, is as pathetic and submissive as she should be, singing her two arias with her customary refinement. The conducting is reliable rather than thrilling.

Recommended alternatives: Tullio Serafin (EMI) – Maria Callas predictably gives even greater profile to Turandot than Nilsson, but the voice becomes squally under pressure. Elisabeth Schwarzkopf, in her only recorded collaboration with Callas, is a moving if unidiomatic Liù; Eugenio Fernandi is a strikingly fine Calaf. Zubin Mehta (Decca) – casting against the grain proves interesting here with Joan Sutherland undertaking a part she would not have attempted on stage, Montserrat Caballé as an almost too refined Liù, and Pavarotti as a resplendent Calaf. Sir John Barbirolli (EMI) – extracts from a 1937 performance at Covent Garden on one CD enshrine a memento of Eva Turner's famous portrayal of Turandot, with the legendary Giovanni Martinelli as an intense Calaf – not to be overlooked.

Gustav Charpentier (1860–1956)

Louise. Ileana Cotrubas (Louise), Jane Berbié (Mother), Placido Domingo (Julien), Gabriel Bacquier (Father), Ambrosian Opera Ch, New Philharmonia O/Georges Prêtre. (Sony CD 46429)

When first written this piece was notable, among other qualities, for its then-shocking portrayal of 'free love' in 1900 Paris: Louise, the naive seamstress daughter of upright working-class Parisians, is torn apart by her love for Julien, a neighbouring poet, who is handsome but lazy. She goes to live with him, but returns home when her beloved father falls ill. Eventually she defies her parents and goes back to Julien to the fury of her father, who pours scorn on the loose morals of the young. *Plus ça change. . . .*

Tristan harmonies and Puccinian motifs inform this picture of young love in Bohemian Paris. The score is richly orchestrated and full of passionate music, including the heroine's elevating 'Depuis le jour', often recorded separately. On the Sony set Cotrubas vividly depicts Louise's innocence and charm; Domingo is a more anonymous, but golden-throated Julien. Best of the three principals is Bacquier as the Father. His is undoubtedly the plum part: he makes the most of it. The many cameo roles, representing Parisian citizens and eccentrics, are taken with varying success by British singers of the day (1976).

In the 1930s a famous set of substantial extracts was recorded with Ninon Vallin in the title role and Georges Thill as Julien. This has just been reissued on CD by Nimbus.

Claude Debussy (1862–1918)

Pelléas et Mélisande. Colette Alliot-Lugaz (Mélisande), Jocelyne Taillon (Geneviève), Didier Henry (Pelléas), Gilles Cachemaille (Golaud), Pierre Thau (Arkel), Montreal Symphony O/Charles Dutoit. (Decca 430 502-2)

Maeterlinck's play is the inspiration for Debussy's sole masterpiece in the genre. He set the text virtually as it stood, finding the perfect musical equivalent for its strange story of love, jealousy and betrayal in the mysterious land of the imaginary Allemonde where time seems to stand still and everything occurs in a half light. The work is written in a sustained and heightened recitative style, the notes responding minutely to the detailed emotions of the text. The sensuous, intimate vocal line is underpinned by Debussy's mastery at evoking inner moods and outer atmospheres in his rich yet delicately patterned score. The story tells of the illicit love of the mysterious, winsome Mélisande for Pelléas, the half-brother of Golaud, her husband, who found her alone and seemingly in a wood. When Golaud finds Pelléas kissing Mélisande in the garden, he kills her in an uncontrollable fit of jealousy. The mood of unstated fear and mysterious depths is sustained from beginning to end.

This, the work's most recent recording, is worthy of the piece. Dutoit and his splendid orchestra, truthfully recorded, catch all the wondrous colour and beauty of the score, also its mood of underlying passions and doubts. Essential in this work is a Francophone cast such as that assembled here. Alliot-Lugaz suggests all Mélisande's attraction and fey, equivocal nature, and sings with greater warmth than the traditional Mélisande. Henry is a properly youthful, eager, palpitating Pelléas. Cachemaille is a forthright, vivid and anguished Golaud. Thau, as the boys' father, is suitably grave and deep-toned.

Recommended alternatives: Roger Desormière (EMI) – this set, recorded in wartime Paris in 1941, remains a classic with perhaps the most telling cast ever to have committed the work to disc. Irène Joachim's withdrawn, fragile Mélisande, Jacques Jansen's luminously sung Pelléas, Henri Etcheverry's marvellously intense Golaud, Germaine Cernay's dignified Geneviève (eloquent in her letter-reading scene) and Paul Cabanel's sonorous Arkel are supported by Desormière's profound understanding of the score gained over many years conducting it in the theatre. Ernest Ansermet's two versions (Decca), particularly the first, are worth hearing: the first is due out on CD in the near future. A brand-new set from DG, conducted by Claudio Abbado, is notable for its scrupulous attention to detail and for François Le Roux's palpitating Pelléas, but it hasn't quite the natural atmosphere of the Dutoit.

Pietro Mascagni (1863–1945) and Ruggiero Leoncavallo (1858–1919)

(i) *Cavalleria Rusticana.* (MASCAGNI); (ii) *Pagliacci* (LEONCAVALLO).
1. (i) Julia Varady (Santuzza), Carmen Gonzales (Lola), Ida Bormida (Mamma Lucia), Luciano Pavarotti (Turiddu), Piero Cappuccilli (Alfio), London Voices, National Philharmonic O/Gianandrea Gavazzeni.
(ii) Mirella Freni (Nedda), Luciano Pavarotti (Canio), Vincenzo Bello (Beppe), Lorenzo Saccomani (Silvio), Ingvar Wixell (Tonio), London Voices, National Philharmonic O/ Giuseppe Patanè. (Decca 414 590-2 (two operas on two CDs))
2. (i) Fiorenza Cossotto (Santuzza), Adriana Martino (Lola), Anna di Stasio (Mamma Lucia), Carlo Bergonzi (Turiddu),

Giangiacomo Guelfi (Alfio), Ch and O of La Scala, Milan/
Herbert von Karajan.
(ii) Joan Carlyle (Nedda), Carlo Bergonzi (Canio), Ugo
Benelli (Beppe), Rolando Panerai (Silvio), Giuseppe Taddei
(Tonio), Ch and O of La Scala, Milan. And *Opera Intermezzi*.
O of La Scala, Milan/Herbert von Karajan. (DG 419 257-2
(three CDs))

Cav and *Pag*, as they are affectionately known, have been virtually
inseparable partners almost since they first appeared. Both works
represent the epitome of what is known as *verismo*, that is operas
relating every day events in the lives of ordinary people, a new
concept in Italian opera at the end of the nineteenth century. Both
operas deal with passions, jealousy and revenge in close-knit
communities; the first set in a Sicilian village, the second in a
Calabrian town. In *Cav*, Turiddu, Santuzza's cavalier boyfriend,
has deserted her for the sensual Lola, wife of the teamster Alfio.
When Alfio discovers her infidelity from Santuzza he demands a
duel with Turiddu (the Rustic Chivalry of the title) and slays his
rival. In the second, which concerns a travelling *commedia dell'arte*
troupe, Nedda is married to the older Canio, head of the troupe.
When he discovers Nedda's affair with the young, handsome
Silvio, he murders her during a performance, then attacks Silvio,
who is in the audience. Nedda is betrayed by the vicious, jealous
hunchback Tonio, who has himself been rejected by Nedda. So the
two stories follow similar lines.

Karajan's grandly conceived, superbly played, and intensely
sung performances are classics and remain so, the 1960s recording hardly dated at all, but his leisurely tempi mean that the two
operas stretch over three CDs. Bergonzi sings with splendid fire
and stylish phrasing in both tenor parts, even if Canio is slightly
too heavy for him. Cossotto is an impassioned Santuzza. Guelfi,
Panerai and Taddei bring idiomatic tone and diction to their
respective roles. The more recent versions, on two CDs, with
Pavarotti in both tenor parts are more tautly conducted and just
as thrilling as the Karajan versions. Although some of the
subsidiary casting is less than ideal, Varady is a committed
Santuzza, moulding her music with refined phrasing and vibrant
tone and Freni is a suitably Italianate and keen-voiced Nedda.

PIETRO MASCAGNI and RUGGIERO LEONCAVALLO ————

Recommended alternatives: Tullio Serafin (EMI) – the mono performances of both works, on three CDs, feature Callas in vivid portrayals of Santuzza and Nedda, nicely differentiated, and Giuseppe di Stefano at his most involved as Turiddu and Canio. *Pag* is further distinguished by Tito Gobbi's acutely portrayed Tonio and Panerai's sensuous singing as Silvio. Renato Cellini (EMI, *Pag* only) – this performance has Victoria de los Angeles as a lovely Nedda and Jussi Björling as a stylish Canio.

L'amico Fritz (MASCAGNI). Mirella Freni (Suzel), Luciano Pavarotti (Fritz Kobus), Vincente Sardinero (David), Ch and O of Royal Opera House, Covent Garden/Gianandrea Gavazzeni. (EMI CDS7 47905-8)

This is the only complete recording of an opera Pavarotti made for EMI before he was signed exclusively by Decca in the 1960s. The tenor's then light, lyrical voice and fervent manner ideally suited the role of shy Fritz, a rich bachelor landowner. This pastoral comedy concerns Fritz, the professional matchmaker Rabbi David, and the beautiful farmer's daughter Suzel. Pavarotti and his fellow-Modenese, Mirella Freni (they shared the same wet nurse!) as an utterly delightful Suzel make a convincing case for this slight but charming opera, at the very opposite end of the emotional spectrum from the over-heated *Cav*, although it was written only a year (1891) after its more famous predecessor.

Iris (MASCAGNI). Ilona Tokody (Iris), Placido Domingo (Osaka), Juan Pons (Kyoto), Bonaldo Giaiotti (Blind Man), Bavarian Radio Ch, Munich Radio O/Giuseppe Patanè. (CBS/Sony CD 45526)

Set in nineteenth-century Japan, this work (1898) tells of the vain attempt by Osaka to win the love of the pure young Iris. He arranges with Kyoto, a brothel-keeper, to have her abducted. Her blind father, thinking she has gone there voluntarily, curses her. She drowns herself in a sewer. This unsavoury story is set by Mascagni with skill and a good deal of sympathy, especially in such a convincing performance as this. Tokody, a much underrated Hungarian soprano, is a moving Iris, Domingo a passionate Osaka, Pons a saturnine Kyoto.

Richard Strauss (1864–1949)

Salome. Cheryl Studer (Salome), Leonie Rysanek (Herodias), Clemens Bieber (Narraboth), Horst Hiestermann (Herod), Bryn Terfel (Jokanaan), O of the Deutschen Oper, Berlin/ Giuseppe Sinopoli. (DG 431 810-2)

Strauss's setting of a German translation of Oscar Wilde's play was his first major success in the opera house. Its musical setting in colours, harmonies and textures that were bold, original and erotically explicit caused a sensation. Even today they have lost little of their power to stimulate controversy as to whether they are thrillingly vivid or merely vulgar and/or sensational. A satisfactory performance, while exposing the wonderfully immediate detail of Strauss's writing, shouldn't degenerate into the blatant. Discipline and control should be the order of the day – as in Sinopoli's sensuous, strongly delineated and resplendently recorded version.

The main glory of this DG set is Studer's representation of the spoilt, wilful, determined Princess, who demands and eventually gets the head of Jokanaan (John the Baptist) on a platter as reward for her striptease (Dance of the Seven Veils) performed before her neurotic stepfather Herod and her raddled mother Herodias. In her perfectly timed and contoured performance, Studer fulfils all the inordinate demands Strauss places on his protagonist in a reading that boxes the compass in terms of tonal variety and histrionic characterisation. She is at once the demanding child, the young girl obsessed with her sexual awakening, and at the end the woman destroyed by her desire to possess Jokanaan. Strauss would have loved Studer's ability to lighten her voice to encompass his often delicate writing and at the same time her reserves of power allow her to ride over the orchestra in the climaxes, culminating in a riveting account of the long finale.

As the visionary Jokanaan, oblivious to Salome's attractions, Bryn Terfel strikes the right note of firm, declamatory vigour. Hiestermann is properly neurotic as Herod but doesn't always sing steadily. Rysanek, once herself a famed Salome, is a rightly cynical Herodias. The smaller parts are all well taken. The recording is spacious.

Recommended alternative: Sir Georg Solti (Decca) – this famous version has stood the test of time. Solti may occasionally overheat the score, but he draws from the Vienna Philharmonic playing of ravishing beauty and tremendous strength. Birgit Nilsson offers a vitally characterised, gloriously sung Salome, only a notch below Studer's as a convincing interpretation. Eberhard Waechter is a single-minded, fanatical Jokanaan. Gerhard Stolze's Herod is almost too vividly characterised. Don't miss the unforgettable reading of the Final Scene by Ljuba Welitsch, the finest Salome of all, in her 1944 version, part of a Welitsch recital (EMI). The video/laserdisc with Teresa Stratas as Salome, conducted by Karl Böhm and produced by Götz Friedrich, is worth investigating.

> *Elektra.* Birgit Nilsson (Elektra), Marie Collier (Chrysothemis), Regina Resnik (Clytemnestra), Gerhard Stolze (Aegisth), Tom Krause (Orest), Vienna Philharmonic O/Sir Georg Solti. (Decca 417 345-2)

The ghost of Agamemnon, the mythological Greek king slain by his wife Clytemnestra and her paramour Aegisthus, pervades this, perhaps the most searching, certainly the most tragically grand of all Strauss's operas. Here, in 1909, he was among the avant garde, relentlessly moving forward the boundaries of harmony, orchestral colour, textural concentration and psychological insight as expressed in music. After it Strauss turned away from modernism towards the calmer regions of *Der Rosenkavalier.* The intensity of mood and composition are maintained from start to finish in this 100-minute plus, one-act drama, with the obsessed and single-minded Elektra, intent to revenge her father's murder.

Solti, always at his most convincing in Strauss, conducts a high-voltage performance sustaining tension and excitement throughout the unbroken length of the work, here given complete as seldom happens in the theatre. Nilsson gives a truly inspired, unflinching performance of the title role, for which her tireless and incisive voice are ideally suited. At the same time she brings variety of tone and timbre to express Elektra's changing moods. Marie Collier, as Chrysothemis, Elektra's sister longing for a normal life with husband and child, sounds properly over-wrought, frustrated and unable to cope with her claustrophobic, doom-laden surroundings. Resnik's Clytemnestra is a raddled, neurotic figure whose nightmares prove all too true. Krause makes a strong, implacable agent of revenge so one wishes his part were longer. Stolze offers a typically detailed cameo as Aegisth. John Culshaw's highly imaginative recording adds to the set's success even if it sometimes goes over the top.

Recommended alternatives: Wolfgang Sawallisch (EMI) – a somewhat more restrained and consistent reading (complete) than Solti's with emphasis on the long view rather than momentary excitement. Eva Marton is a powerful, almost manic Elektra, Cheryl Studer a lyrical Chysothemis, Marjana Lipovšek a more plausible Clytemnestra than Resnik. Seiji Ozawa (Philips) – a subtle, almost too sensuous performance (making traditional cuts) featuring Hildegard Behrens as the most sympathetic and psychologically interesting of Elektras and Christa Ludwig as a regal, overbearing Clytemnestra. All three versions are worth consideration for their singular attributes. On video/laserdisc, Leonie Rysanek's assumption of the title role is riveting in Friedrich's expressionist production, authoritatively conducted by Böhm (Decca).

Der Rosenkavalier. Hilde Gueden (Sophie), Maria Reining (Marschallin), Sena Jurinac (Octavian), Hilde Rössl-Majdan (Annina), Anton Dermota (Italian Singer), Peter Klein (Valzacchi), Alfred Poell (Faninal), Ludwig Weber (Baron Ochs), Vienna State Opera Ch, Vienna Philharmonic/Erich Kleiber. (Decca 425 950-2, mono)

This historic set, recorded in 1954, has yet to be surpassed as an all-round performance of Strauss's romantic-comic masterpiece. It represents rewardingly the way this work was performed in Vienna at what can now be seen as the end of a treasured tradition. In it every role, down to the smallest, is the product of a close-knit ensemble now no longer in existence. That tradition depended on conductors regularly working with the same singers to achieve a consistent style of performance. Erich Kleiber was, however, more than a mere conductor of tradition: he was a genius at lighting Strauss's music from within, giving its waltzes a wonderful lift, and illuminating the small details in which this score abounds. Kleiber was careful never to linger, as so many of his successors have done, over the more expressive passages, never allowing sentiment to fall over into sentimentality. Thus the affair between the Marschallin and her youthful lover Octavian is never overplayed even though the passions being delineated are real enough nor does Ochs here become either a boor or a bore, while the pure love of Octavian for young Sophie, the nouveau-riche Faninal's pretty daughter, is presented with loving care.

Maria Reining, the Marschallin, was by 1954 nearing the end of a distinguished career as an eminent Straussian. Though her tone may no longer be as fresh as one might wish, she consoles us for any deficiency by her profound understanding of the role, demonstrated in her clear diction, impeccable phrasing and genuine, idiomatic characterisation. Jurinac had precisely the voice, soprano with a warm lower register, that Strauss surely envisaged for Octavian. She is wonderfully ardent and impulsive in the part and, when disguised as the maid Mariandel, never overplays the comedy. Gueden's silvery tones are ideal for Sophie's high-lying music and she shows the right mettle in her vocal acting: this Sophie is no shrinking violet. Weber's Viennese accent, his play with words, and his rich voice give to Ochs just the right profile, overweening, fun-loving, a shade pompous, but never vulgar. The smaller parts, not least Poell's fussing Faninal, are taken by ensemble players of long experience. The recording, though in mono, catches the strengths of a vintage period in the VPO's history. The score is uncut.

Recommended alternatives: Sir Georg Solti (Decca) – this 1970s set (uncut), often underrated, houses Régine Crespin's sincere, mellow Marschallin, a secure Octavian in Yvonne Minton, Helen Donath's clear-voiced Sophie, Manfred Jungwirth's amusing Ochs, all supported by Solti's clear-eyed reading. Herbert von Karajan (EMI) – this much-vaunted set of 1956 (stereo) has Elisabeth Schwarzkopf as a seasoned, somewhat mannered Marschallin and Christa Ludwig as a committed Octavian and the vintage Philharmonia giving Strauss's score a warm glow, under Karajan's leisurely direction. (He makes the traditional cuts.) Robert Heger (abridged set, recorded 1933, EMI) – this pioneering effort preserves Lotte Lehmann's classic Marschallin, Elisabeth Schumann's silvery Sophie and Richard Mayr's wonderfully ripe Ochs. On laserdisc – Carlos Kleiber (DG) – son of Erich, Carlos inherited his father's genius for conducting this work. His is an exhilarating reading taken from the stage of the Bavarian State Opera in Munich (1981), a famous production by Otto Schenk with Gwyneth Jones (Marschallin), Brigitte Fassbaender (Octavian), Lucia Popp (Sophie) and Jungwirth (Ochs) all giving rounded portrayals with an ensemble-like integration. Sound and picture are superb, a wonderful advertisement for a new medium.

> *Ariadne auf Naxos.* Rita Streich (Zerbinetta), Elisabeth Schwarzkopf (Ariadne), Irmgard Seefried (Composer), Rudolf Schock (Bacchus), Hugues Cuenod (Dancing Master), Karl Dönch (Music Teacher), Philharmonia O/Herbert von Karajan. (EMI CMS7 69296-2 (mono))

This work began life in 1912 as a one-act opera to be played after Hoffmannsthal's abridged version of Molière's *Le Bourgeois gentilhomme* for which Strauss wrote the incidental music. In the revised, more practical version (1916), the opera is preceded by a musical Prologue depicting the events before it was staged. This new version allowed Strauss to create one of his most endearing, sympathetic characters, the Composer. In the opera proper the soulful, romantic musings of Ariadne, in isolation on Naxos before being rescued by Bacchus, are contrasted with the brilliance of the *commedia dell'arte* troupe headed by Zerbinetta, sung by a *coloratura* soprano, who has a long, complex aria.

The 1954 performance is a classic. Seefried is an impetuous, warm-hearted Composer, Schwarzkopf a dignified, moving Ariadne, Streich a nimble never brittle Zerbinetta, Schock an ardent Bacchus. Smaller roles are filled by lively, characterful singers; Karajan's direction is masterly over all and in detail. Walter Legge's production is exemplary.

Recommended alternatives: Kurt Masur (Philips) – well-integrated modern version with Jessye Norman as a rather grand Ariadne, Julia Varady a fiery Composer. Karl Böhm (DG) – historic performance recorded live in Vienna to honour Strauss' eightieth birthday in 1944 with Maria Reining as the best of all Ariadnes, Seefried at twenty-four at the start of her illustrious career in wonderfully fresh form, Alda Noni a sparkling Zerbinetta, Max Lorenz an exuberant Bacchus. Video/laserdisc version with

Norman again as Ariadne, conducted by James Levine (DG), is somewhat overblown.

Die Frau ohne Schatten. Leonie Rysanek (Empress), Christel Goltz (Dyer's Wife), Elisabeth Hoengen (Nurse), Hans Hopf (Emperor), Paul Schoeffler (Barak), Vienna State Opera Ch, Vienna Philharmonic O/Karl Böhm. (Decca 425 981-2)

This vast fairy-tale-cum-allegory was the most ambitious, anti-Straussians would say most pretentious, project Strauss and his librettist Hugo von Hofmannsthal ever undertook. It attempts an overview of the human condition in terms of an Eastern-inspired fantasy concerning the contact of mortals with supernatural beings and forces. The score is the most complex ever attempted even by Strauss and it stretches over three long acts, almost always foreshortened in the theatre and on disc (but see below). This version, longer than most heard in the opera house, was the work's first-ever recording, at once a pioneering and inspired effort, owing much to the persistence of Böhm and his dedicated cast, who had been performing the opera in Vienna and persuaded a reluctant Decca to set it on record back in 1956. Nobody knew or loved the piece more than Böhm, whose second recording, 'live' from Vienna on DG, is also worth hearing, not least for Birgit Nilsson's convincing portrayal of the Dyer's Wife.

Having worked together on stage, the singers on the Decca set all suggest by vocal means alone that they are inside their roles. The young Rysanek is appropriately ethereal and in Act 3 deeply moving as the Empress who throws no shadow, symbol that she is barren. Her dilemma is that she can gain a shadow only at the expense of the Dyer's Wife on earth. The part calls for just the kind of soaring, lyrical soprano Rysanek possessed. As the more earthy Dyer's Wife, a frustrated shrew, willing to give up her shadow for promised riches, Goltz, although sometimes wobbly, is a proper termagant, later illumined by deeper feelings. As her long-suffering husband Barak, Schoeffler radiates warmth and sympathy, his utterance intense and eloquent. Nobody could fail to be moved by his singing. The Emperor, another of Strauss's ungrateful parts for a heroic tenor, is strongly but not very communicatively sung by Hopf. The great mezzo Elisabeth Hoengen is the incarnation of evil as the manipulative Nurse. The

VPO, in a golden period, plays with unstinting warmth and vitality. The early stereo recording still sounds respectable; indeed you can hear more of the score than on either of the more gratefully recorded modern sets.

Recommended alternative: Wolfgang Sawallisch (EMI) – this recent set, giving the score complete, has much to commend it, not least Sawallisch's sober command of the work's intricacies. Cheryl Studer is an Empress to match Rysanek's in vocal resplendence, although she is not so involved in her role. Hanna Schwarz is a superbly malevolent Nurse, but the other roles are not taken with as much conviction as on the Decca set.

Arabella. Julia Varady (Arabella), Helen Donath (Zdenka), Helga Schmidt (Adelaide), Adolf Dallapozza (Matteo), Dietrich Fischer-Dieskau (Mandryka), Walter Berry (Count Waldner), Bavarian State Opera Ch and O/Wolfgang Sawallisch. (Orfeo C 169882 H)

This work was the product of the final collaboration between Strauss and Hofmannsthal. They were hoping to achieve a lighter piece, possibly an operetta, but ended up with quite a serious love story where the mettlesome heroine Arabella is searching for the 'right man' and finds him in Mandryka, an outspoken, rich landowner, son of an old friend of her father, Count Waldner. The situation is, however, complicated by Arabella's younger sister, Zdenka, who has been brought up as a boy to save funds by the impecunious Waldner. By a ruse, this frustrated girl manages to spend an illicit night with her beloved Matteo by pretending she is Arabella whom *he* loves. This leads to inevitable confusion, but all turns out well in the end, but not before Mandryka has threatened Matteo with a duel.

The piece nicely balances the comic with the romantic. Sawallisch, that most convinced of today's Straussians, directs a warmhearted, clear-headed account of this appealing if uneven score, keenly supportive – as ever – of his singers. Varady is no shrinking violet of an Arabella, but a girl with a mind of her own. Fischer-Dieskau contributes a predictably well-varied and credible picture of the shy yet formidable Mandryka. He and Varady, real-life husband and wife, make the most of the glorious love duet at the start of Act 2. In all the misunderstandings later in this act and in Act 3, they act astutely with their voices. Helen Donath's silvery soprano is well fitted to Zdenka's high-lying music; Berry makes a crusty, lovable Waldner.

Recommended alternative: Sir Georg Solti (Decca) – this version, now in Decca's 'Historic' series, comes from the early days of stereo (1957) and houses Lisa della Casa's classic interpretation of the title role, securely and beautifully sung. George London is a rightly impulsive Mandryka. The supporting cast is excellent. Avoid the more recent Decca set where Dame Kiri Te Kanawa is a colourless Arabella.

Capriccio. 1. Elisabeth Schwarzkopf (the Countess), Christa Ludwig (Clairon), Nicolai Gedda (Flamand), Hugues Cuenod (Taupe), Dietrich Fischer-Dieskau (Olivier), Eberhard Waechter (the Count), Hans Hotter (La Roche), Philharmonia O/Wolfgang Sawallisch. (EMI CDS7 49014-8 (mono))
2. Gundula Janowitz (the Countess), Tatiana Troyanos (Clairon), Peter Schreier (Flamand), David Thaw (Taupe), Hermann Prey (Olivier), Dietrich Fischer-Dieskau (the Count), Karl Ridderbusch (La Roche), Bavarian Radio Symphony O/Karl Böhm. (DG 419 023-2)

Strauss's last opera is entitled a 'Conversation Piece'. The libretto by Clemens Krauss, who conducted the première in 1943, discusses the relative importance of words and music in opera. The two sides of the argument are personified by the poet Olivier and the composer Flamand. In a neat symmetry both are in love with the lovely Countess Madeleine who cannot choose between them. At the end, after a long and impassioned solo, sometimes recorded on its own, we are left in the air not knowing which of them has won her heart – and similarly not knowing whether the text or the score is the more important. The action takes place in the context of a rehearsal for a play at the Countess's castle near Paris in which the Parisian actress Clairon is acting. She is an old flame of Olivier's now loved by the Countess's brother. Strauss and Krauss keep this closely woven plot on its feet with the lightest of touches. The work, though never by its nature likely to be popular in the wider sense, has always had a dedicated following and wins adherents who are willing to take the trouble to understand the libretto. Besides the fascination of the subject and the beauty of the music, the opera is delightful for its variety of characterisation, which includes the cynical old theatre director La Roche, a pair of parodied Italian singers and the small, endearing role of Monsieur Taupe, the prompter.

It is impossible to choose between its only two recordings to date, neither of them new, but both in their different ways will give long-lasting pleasure. Walter Legge assembled what was an EMI house team to record it in 1957, headed by his wife Schwarzkopf as a sophisticated and charming Countess. She is wooed by the most attractive of suitors in Gedda's Flamand and Fischer-Dieskau's Olivier. Ludwig is a glowing Clairon, Waechter a handsome-voiced Count. Perhaps best of all is Hotter's marvellously characterised La Roche. Sawallisch has the whole score bubbling effortlessly along with the detail all clearly exposed. Böhm's reading is slightly more serious-minded with Janowitz a more withdrawn but affecting Countess addressed by excellent suitors. This DG version has the advantage of stereo sound. A lifetime's delight is to be found in either.

Hans Pfitzner (1869–1949)

Palestrina. Helen Donath (Ighino), Brigitte Fassbaender (Silla), Nicolai Gedda (Palestrina), Dietrich Fischer-Dieskau (Cardinal Borromeo), Bernd Weikl (Cardinal Morone), Tölz Boys' Choir, Bavarian Radio Ch, Bavarian Radio Symphony O/Rafael Kubelik. (DG 427 417-2)

A much-honoured composer and theorist in his lifetime, Pfitzner is nowadays remembered largely for this important opera. It has what has sometimes been termed the most significant libretto of any opera in the repertory, one that could virtually be staged as a play, so intelligently is it laid out and so cogently argued. The story concerns, in private (Acts 1 and 3), the trials and tribulations of the renowned sixteenth-century composer of the title, and in public (Act 2) the disputations of the Council of Trent, with its main personalities most pertinently characterised. The portrait of

Palestrina, a man who has lost his inspiration after the death of his wife, is a poignant one. At last he produces the Mass demanded of him by his great friend, Cardinal Borromeo, through mystical communion with the masters of the past – the scene depicting this is unique in opera. As a whole the score, though heavily influenced by Wagner, has its own individual, not to say idiosyncratic cut; perhaps a work for festivals rather than the regular repertory.

Here it receives a worthy performance under Kubelik's commanding, sympathetic baton. Gedda sings fluently although he misses the special, elevated quality of his predecessors, Karl Erb and Julius Patzak, and of his successor, Peter Schreier. Fischer-Dieskau is a formidable Borromeo and the supporting cast is admirable – as is the recording. There exist off-the-air performances featuring Patzak as Palestrina and Hans Hotter as Borromeo, an unbeatable partnership in this music. Should either appear on CD, it would have to be the recommendation.

Franz Lehár (1870–1948)

Die lustige Witwe (The Merry Widow). Elisabeth Schwarz-kopf (Hanna Glawari), Hanny Steffek (Valencienne), Nicolai Gedda (Camille Rosillon), Eberhard Waechter (Graf Danilo), Joseph Knapp (Baron Mirko Zeta), Philharmonia Ch and O/ Lovro von Matačić. (EMI CDS7 47178-8)

Once considered merely a musical comedy, and played and cast as such, this ever-popular work, dating from 1905, has been elevated in recent times to something worthy of the attention of opera singers and distinguished conductors, by virtue of its refined writing for both voice and orchestra. Fresh in note and concept, it always delights an audience in any half-decent performance. Even so it has received remarkably few recordings that do it justice. The old Columbia LP version of 1962 from which these CDs derive comes closest to it. Von Matačić was a conductor much admired by producer Walter Legge, and he here lavishes all the care on the *Widow* that he brought to a Bruckner symphony. He gives the faster numbers irresistible lift and the more sentimental ones a nuance that enhances their status; for instance, Hanna's Vilja-

Lied is subtly done. With the Philharmonia in its vintage heyday, the playing has a bright insouciance and an aristocratic flair that is entirely appropriate.

Those characteristics also inform the singing. Schwarzkopf's Hanna, which had also graced an earlier EMI version (also now on CD) is wonderfully gay and spontaneous, sophisticated and elating; here she epitomises the word allure. By her side Waechter is a slightly hearty Danilo, a baritone where the composer stipulated a tenor, but his portrait of the wayward, playboy embassy *attaché* has the authentic touch to it. Even better is Gedda as the romantic Camille. (His performance in the earlier version was one of his first on record.) Steffek is an ideal Valencienne, a vibrant soprano with plenty of sensuous charm. The whole company is in the same class and so is the recording. Knapp makes an amusing Baron Zeta, whose wife Valencienne is having an affair with Camille, but whose reputation is saved by Hanna. The set excludes the 'Zauber der Hauslichkeit' duet and the cake-walk, included in the set mentioned below.

Recommended alternative: Heinz Wallberg (EMI) – this is a pleasing, relatively modern (1980) version, sympathetically conducted. Edda Moser is a correct rather than alluring Hanna, Hermann Prey a heavily baritone but knowledgeable Danilo. The main honours here go to the delightful Helen Donath as Valencienne and the lyrical Siegfried Jerusalem as Camille. Benno Kusche is an experienced, characterful Baron Zeta.

Maurice Ravel (1875–1937)

(i) *L'Heure Espagnole.* Jane Berbié (Concepción), Jean Giraudeau (Torquemada), Gabriel Bacquier (Ramiro), José van Dam (Don Inigo Gomez)
(ii) *L'Enfant et les sortilèges.* Françoise Ogéas (Child), Silvaine Gilma (Fire, Princess, Nightingale), Jane Berbié (Sofa, She Cat, Squirrel), Colette Herzog (Bat, Little Owl, Shepherdess), Janine Collard (Mother, Chinese Cup, Dragonfly), Michel Sénéchal (Teapot, Little Old Man [Mr Arithmetic]), Camille Maurane (Grandfather Clock, Tom Cat), Heinz

Rehfuss (Armchair, Tree), Ch and Children's Voices of French Radio, French Radio National O/Lorin Maazel. (DG 423 718/9-2)

These two pieces, each a delight and each lasting about 45 minutes, are often paired together on stage, the witty cynicism of the one offset by the fairy-tale ingenuity and child-like fantasy of the other, although their creation was separated by fourteen years. For *The Spanish Hour*, Ravel chose a tale by Franc-Nohain about Concepción, the bored wife of the clockmaker Torquemada, whose regular admirers, poet Gonzalve and portly banker Don Inigo, prove so inadequate, that she turns to Ramiro, the virile muleteer. He has helped her carry large clocks, containing the other two, up to her bedroom. When they fail to provide what she wants, she persuades Ramiro into her boudoir. The libretto is as graceful as it is witty, and the same can be said of Ravel's libretto, which conjures up Spain, clocks and sensuality with equal aplomb.

The Child and the Spells, to a libretto by Colette, concerns another bored creature, this time a small boy who takes out his frustration on the inanimate objects and pets around him. To his surprise they come to life and take their revenge on him. However, he redeems himself by helping a wounded squirrel and when the child also gets hurt, the animals take him home, away from the enchanted garden. Ravel finds precisely the right tone in a score of refined and magical sensitivity and wit, in which sophistication, fantasy and fun are all seamlessly combined.

Happily, in the early 1960s, Maazel, adept in this kind of music, recorded both pieces with casts of singers who fit their roles to perfection. In the first Berbié is the exasperated young wife to the life, Sénéchal the poet with his head in the clouds, van Dam the fatuous banker, Bacquier the simple, bemused muleteer. In the second piece, a whole team of characterful singing-actors, enunciating their native French to the manner trained, bring to life the child and his many friendly tormentors. With a French orchestra in support and an ideally balanced recording, both these discs are a treat.

Manuel de Falla (1876–1946)

La Vida Breve. Victoria de los Angeles (Salud), Carlo Cossutta
(Paco), Orfeon Donostiarra Ch, Spanish National O/Rafael
Frühbeck de Burgos. (EMI CMS7 69590-2)

Falla's torrid melodrama, dating from 1904–5 (though not performed until 1913), is set in Granada. It tells roughly the same tale
as Mascagni's *Cavalleria rusticana* (qv), one of a lover's uncaring
infidelity. Here Paco throws over the gypsy Salud for the more
conventional Carmela. At the wedding of Paco and Carmela,
Salud denounces Paco and falls dead at his feet. Curtain. Falla's
economic writing is imbued with Spanish feeling derived from
folk music and dances. It offers a rewarding role for a soprano able
to encompass Salud's many emotions. Its most telling interpreter
in modern times has been Victoria de los Angeles, who brings to
it here all her gifts for lyrical expression and poignant declamation. Cossutta, with exactly the right voice for the callous Paco,
does what he can for a somewhat cardboard character. Frühbeck
de Burgos draws all the deep emotions and fire from Falla's
powerful writing. The elderly recording is more than adequate.

Béla Bartók (1881–1945)

Duke Bluebeard's Castle. Elena Obraztsova (Judith), Yevgeny
Nesterenko (Bluebeard), Hungarian State Opera Ch and O/
János Ferencsik. (Hungaroton HCD 12254)

Bartók's single-act opera has a libretto by the Symbolist poet Béla
Balázs which tells of Bluebeard introducing his most recent wife
to his palace, where she discovers doors which she unlocks one by
one to find behind them his former wives incarcerated and in
thrall to Bluebeard. The story is usually seen as a psychological
struggle between Bluebeard and Judith, man and wife, but it also
has elements of a mysterious myth. In the theatre it exerts a
magnetic sense of unease. Bartók clothed the piece, first given in
1918, in vivid orchestration, at once colourful and deeply expressive, over which two voices of appreciable strength need to carry.
On disc, most of the difficulties are more easily surmounted. The
creators intended a spoken prologue, announcing that the

audience will see a myth enacted; this has been omitted on most recordings. The vocal parts are on the whole reticent; the real music-drama is played out in the orchestra, where the undercurrents of feeling can be truly felt.

Ferencsik has always had a close affinity with the work, and brings out all aspects of the many-faceted score – the glorious blaze when the fifth door opens is a brilliant moment – as it should be. His Hungarian orchestra brings detailed knowledge of the score to bear on its faithful execution. All in all this is an accurate account of a complicated work. The quieter moments are beautifully realised. Here is unmistakable authenticity. Nesterenko is an authoritative and committed Bluebeard. As Judith, Obraztsova goes over the top at times, but she certainly conveys the female power with which Judith gradually controls Bluebeard.

Recommended alternative: István Kertész – Christa Ludwig and Walter Berry, wife and husband in real life at the time this set was recorded back in the mid 1960s, sing their roles with tremendous panache, catching the interaction of the antagonists perhaps more successfully than any other on disc, although the performance isn't as vocally idiomatic or as accurate as the Hungarian one. The London Symphony Orchestra play splendidly for their then-music director and the recording still sounds well.

Igor Stravinsky (1882–1971)

Oedipus Rex. Shirley Verrett (Jocasta), George Shirley (Oedipus), Lorin Driscoll (Shepherd), John Reardon (Messenger), Donald Gramm (Creon), Chester Watson (Tiresias), John Westbrook (Narrator), Washington Opera Society Ch and O/Igor Stravinsky. (Sony CD 46290)

Stravinsky intended this taut, hieratical piece, which he termed an 'opera-oratorio', to be staged, and when given in the opera house it makes an overwhelming impression. The deliberate distancing effect of the Latin text and a Narrator intervening to advance the story in the vernacular always proves riveting. The ritual enactment of the terrible tragedy is that much more horrific when presented in a dead language – and, of course, it is greatly enhanced by Stravinsky's direct, economical music, one of his most inspired scores, which eventually reaches its inevitable conclusion with awful truthfulness. This recording, the second made by the composer, is only available as part of Sony's 22-CD Stravinsky edition. It is unfortunately the only recommendable rendering now available. (Sony must reissue Stravinsky's earlier version, with Jean Cocteau, who wrote the text, as Narrator, and EMI should reissue its Sadler's Wells version under Colin Davis.) The performance under consideration is stamped with the composer's authority and has a cast of then-young American singers dedicated in their singing. Stravinsky makes sure we feel the full force of his score by virtue of his steady speeds and unfevered but urgent approach.

The Rake's Progress. 1. Cathryn Pope (Anne Trulove), Sarah Walker (Baba the Turk), Astrid Varnay (Mother Goose), Philip Langridge (Tom Rakewell), John Dobson (Sellem), Samuel Ramey (Nick Shadow), Stafford Dean (Trulove), London Sinfonietta and Ch/Riccardo Chailly. (Decca 411 644-2)
2. Judith Raskin (Anne Trulove), Regina Sarfaty (Baba the Turk), Jean Manning (Mother Goose), Alexander Young (Tom Rakewell), Kevin Miller (Sellem), John Reardon (Nick Shadow), Don Garrard (Trulove), Sadler's Wells Opera Ch, Royal Philharmonic O/Igor Stravinsky. (Sony CD 46290)

Stravinsky got the inspiration for this neo-classical opera when he saw Hogarth's cycle of paintings of the same name at the Chicago Art Institute in 1947. He charged W.H. Auden with writing the libretto and Auden in turn called on Chester Kallman to help him complete the job. The result was a highly stylised conceit with apparently cartoon archetypes for characters, but somehow the work itself took over: far from being merely a well-observed, tightly controlled picture, it became a thing of flesh and blood in which, perhaps in spite of ourselves, we become involved in the sad fate of Tom and Anne, and mesmerised by Nick Shadow, devil incarnate by virtue of Stravinsky's genius. The form recalls eighteenth-century style in having recitatives and set numbers, a small orchestra and a neat division among solo, ensemble and chorus, but all are infected with Stravinsky's unmistakable rhythms and harmonies, giving the score, very properly, an individual signature.

The 1985 Decca version cannot quite equal the natural authenticity and flow of the composer's own recording, but the latter comes at present only as part of that 22-CD album of Stravinsky conducting his own works. For the everyday collector wanting the piece in his collection the Chailly will do well enough. Langridge is firstly a flamboyant, then a downtrodden and moving Tom, Cathryn Pope a light and not unappealing Anne (though it is a pity Felicity Lott wasn't engaged for the role). As in Glyndebourne's staging, contemporaneous with this recording, Ramey is a forthright, plausible Shadow. Sarah Walker is a predictably extravagant Baba the Turk, a character of the authors' invention, larger than life, brilliantly characterised in her music. Dean is a sturdy Trulove.

On most counts, they are bettered by the 1961 set made in London and based on performances at Sadler's Wells Opera (though these were not conducted by the composer). Young is a vivid, subtle Tom (said to be the composer's ideal), singing more pleasingly than Langridge, Raskin a more charming Anne than Pope, and Reardon a more saturnine Shadow than Ramey. Chailly conducts well enough, but Stravinsky is the more pointed and astringent advocate of his own music. LPs exist of the 1951 première in Venice, with Schwarzkopf as Anne, but this invaluable document has not yet been transferred to CD.

Alban Berg (1885–1935)

Wozzeck. Hildegard Behrens (Marie), Anna Gonda (Margret), Walter Raffeiner (Drum-Major), Heinz Zednik (Captain), Philip Langridge (Andres), Franz Grundheber (Wozzeck), Aage Haugland (Doctor), Vienna Boys' Choir, Vienna State Opera Chorus, Vienna Philharmonic O/ Claudio Abbado. (DG 423 587-2)

In spite of its structural complexity, which makes it initially as hard to listen to as it is to perform, this work triumphs in the theatre and on disc. This is because of its extraordinary power to move the listener as the composer sympathises with poor

Wozzeck, protagonist of Georg Buchner's play on which the opera's libretto is closely based by the composer himself. Conceived in 1914, work on the score was interrupted by the war; it was eventually completed in 1921 and given its première (after being turned down by most music directors in Germany) at the Berlin State Opera in 1925 under the baton of Erich Kleiber. He also directed the first London performances at Covent Garden in 1952 – but sadly recorded nothing from a score that he did so much to foster.

This live recording, the opera's most recent, was taken direct from performances at the Vienna State Opera during June 1987. Abbado, always a convincing advocate of Berg's music, conducts an urgent, raw reading that seems to tear into the heart of the piece: the inner sorrow of Wozzeck's dire predicament and Berg's implied protest at his treatment by those around him. The performance is at once amazingly accurate and, on the whole, expressively compelling. The pathos and bitterness of Wozzeck himself are poignantly expressed by Grundheber, and Behrens is wonderful at showing the twin extremes of Marie's character – sensual desire before the erotic approaches of the preening Drum-Major, gentle and concerned with her downtrodden child. The smaller roles are all grippingly taken. The fact that this is a 'real' performance in an opera house enhances the feeling of being present at a great tragedy as singers act and react before our ears.

Recommended alternative: Christoph von Dohnanyi (Decca) – this is a thoroughly prepared studio recording under a conductor who knows the score intimately. Eberhard Waechter is a sorrowful, tense, somewhat uneven Wozzeck; Anja Silja a marvellously vivid Marie.

Lulu. Teresa Stratas (Lulu), Yvonne Minton (Countess Geschwitz), Hanna Schwarz (Schoolboy), Kenneth Riegel (Alwa), Robert Tear (Painter, Negro), Franz Mazura (Dr Schön), Toni Blankenheim (Schigolch, Police Officer), Gerd Nienstedt (Animal Trainer, Rodrigo), O of the Paris Opéra/ Pierre Boulez. (DG 415 489-2)

Berg's second and last opera is even more complex than his first. Its ways of composition may be similar, with the emphasis on closed forms; its ethos is quite different, dealing with immorality and death in an offhand, oblique way, with sinister undertones which become much more overt towards the end. The work, to a libretto drawn by the composer from two works by Frank Wedekind, was left unfinished at the time of the composer's untimely death, and given in two-act form at its Zurich première in 1937. It was completed from the composer's substantial sketches by Friedrich Cerha after the death of Berg's widow, and given its full première only in 1979 at the Paris Opéra conducted by Boulez. The recording is based on those performances.

Boulez is to be thanked for the lucidity, clarity and discipline of his reading even if he doesn't achieve the greater intensity of Karl Böhm and Christoph von Dohnányi (with the wonderful Silja in the title role) in their sets of the first two acts, the latter on CD from Decca. Stratas, an alluring Lulu on stage, gives a vibrant portrayal by vocal means alone, even when the role sounds vocally a shade too much for her. The supporting cast is good but in some respects not the equal of those on the earlier sets. Still the arrival of the complete work, so lauded when it happened, is here securely recorded on disc for posterity.

Sergey Prokofiev (1891–1953)

L'amour des trois oranges (The Love for three oranges). Catherine Dubosc (Ninetta), Michèle Lagrange (Fata Morgana), Hélène Perraguin (Princess Clarissa), Béatrice Uria Monzon (Smeraldina), Jean-Luc Viala (Prince), Georges Gautier (Truffaldino), Didier Henry (Pantaloon, Farfarello), Gabriel Bacquier (King of Clubs), Vincent Le Texier (Leandro), Jules Bastin (Cook), Gregory Reinhart (Tchelio), Ch and O of Lyon Opéra/Kent Nagano. (Virgin Classics VCD7 91084-2 [also on video])

Within a *commedia dell'arte* setting after Gozzi, Prokofiev laced his bitter-sweet comedy with a deal of satire at the expense of conventions and authority. The composer's score, to his own libretto, has an apt 1920s edge to it, but it is also full of well-contrived comedy and boasts one memorable tune, the frequently heard March. The Prince's hypochondriac melancholy is lifted at the sight of Fata Morgana tumbling over, in revenge for which she casts a love-spell on him for the three oranges of the title. His search for the oranges lands him in a never-never-land where he encounters, among others, an outsize Cook (sung by a bass), and all kinds of vicissitudes perpetrated by those who wish him ill (they are eventually routed). Two 'oranges' die of heat; the third reveals the beautiful Ninetta, who will be the Prince's future queen.

The recording by Lyon Opéra derives from a marvellous staging there, which can be caught on the well-made video. Young Kent Nagano catches the vivacity of the score and conducts it with zest, ably supported by his orchestra. He is blessed with a cast that includes many of the best Francophone singers of the past decade or so. Gautier, Viala, Henry, Bacquier and Bastin – hilarious as the aforementioned Cook – are only the best of a dedicated band, who enter unitedly into the zany happenings depicted within. A delight all round.

The Fiery Angel. Nadine Secunde (Renata), Heinz Zednik (Mephistophélès), Siegfried Lorenz (Ruprecht), Petteri Salomaa (Faust), Kurt Moll (Inquisitor), Gothenburg Pro Musica Ch, Gothenburg Symphony O/Neeme Järvi. (DG 431 669-2)

This opera followed on the *Oranges*, and has a very different scenario. Here the composer's fantastic strain is turned to horrific ends in a lurid tale of sexual frustration, sorcery and possession, culminating in an exorcism in a convent. This is strictly adult 'entertainment' as compared with the frolics of its predecessor. The libretto, by the composer, is based on a novel by Valeri Brysov, itself based on a love triangle in which the author was involved. The score hovers somewhat uneasily between the depiction of black magic and black humour. Its most successful creation is the central figure of Renata whose obsession with an apparition draws the knight Ruprecht into her life, although even here the composer's approach to his anti-heroine is ambivalent. Although written between 1922 and 1925, the work had to wait thirty years before it was staged.

Whatever one's qualms about the plot, the inventive power and drive of the score, with its steamily insistent atmosphere enhanced by blatant dissonance, carries all before it in a thoroughly prepared performance such as this one conducted by Järvi, a notable proponent of Prokofiev's music. That said, he doesn't always match the full force of the score as his predecessors have done. Secunde has a gallant shot at Renata's taxing role, but wants the authority and variety of Jane Rhodes on an old Decca recording that should be reissued on CD. Similarly Lorenz, as Ruprecht, is effective rather than wholly convincing. These two, like the rest of the cast, aren't quite idiomatic enough in Russian (the older version is sung in French by French singers). An exception to this stricture is Kurt Moll, whose appearance late on as the Inquisitor has the right presence and relish missing elsewhere. As a whole, the set should be heard for its fair representation of one of the century's landmark operas which is still too little known.

War and Peace. Galina Vishnevskaya (Natasha Rostova), Katherine Ciesinski (Sonia), Stefania Toczyska (Helena Bezukhova), Mariana Paunova (Marie Akhrosimova), Mira Zakai (Princess Maria Bolkonsky), Wieslaw Ochman (Piotr Bezukhov), Nicolai Gedda (Prince Anatol Kuragin), Lajos Miller (Prince Andrei Bolkonsky), Nicola Ghiuselev (Marshal Kutuzov), Edward Tumagian (Napoleon Bonaparte), Ch of Radio France, French National O/Mstislav Rostropovich. (Erato 2290-45331-2)

Prokofiev's last and greatest opera was written during the German siege of Russia in 1941–2 and first performed in 1946. Its skill in reducing Tolstoy's vast novel to the bounds of a two-part operatic epic, lasting some four hours when given complete and depicting 72 characters, is astonishing, as he reflects almost every aspect of the story in his chosen episodes, depicting the private and public destinies of its principals against the background of a Russia under threat, as indeed it was at the time of writing. The composer also devised clearly etched and unerringly conceived portraits of Pierre, Kuragin, Natasha, Kutuzov and Napoleon. Of the thirteen scenes the first seven are allotted to Peace, the next six to War, although the latter is by far the more substantial section, at least when the score is presented uncut as it is here. Then the sense of a wide-ranging panorama of war's devastation is keenly felt. The score, Prokofiev's most ambitious, finds the appropriate music for every facet of the story – romantic in Part 1, brutal and often tragic in Part 2.

Rostropovich, who as a young man knew the composer and conducted the work first in 1970, is in command of the huge scenario which he presents with both clarity and commitment in a broadly conceived, fairly free manner. Ochman is an appropriately romantic Pierre, Miller an ardent Andrei, Ghiuselev a magisterial Kutuzov. Gedda creates a devastating cameo of a decadent being as the voluptuous cad Anatol; Toczyska is rightly sensual as his corrupt sister Helena. Most of the smaller roles are well taken. If the great Vishnevskaya recorded the part of Natasha rather too late in her career, we are consoled by her obviously authentic accents for the sometimes hard and unrelenting tone.

The tremendous television performance seen on BBC in 1990, a Covent Garden/Kirov collaboration conducted by Valery Gergiev, will be issued in both sound and vision by Philips within a year or two, but for the moment the Erato set, now at mid-price, will do well enough as a representation of this grand work. Besides the recording does its appreciable best to simulate a stage performance.

George Gershwin (1898–1937)

Porgy and Bess. Cynthia Haymon (Bess), Harolyn Blackwell (Clara), Cynthia Clarey (Serena), Marietta Simpson (Maria), Damon Evans (Sportin' Life), Willard White (Porgy), Gregg Baker (Crown), Glyndebourne Ch, London Philharmonic O/Simon Rattle. (EMI CDS7 49568-2)

Once frowned on by superior persons as merely a show or a glorified musical, Gershwin's multi-faceted score is now accepted as an opera, which deserves to be performed as such. Heard in its entirety, its form, flow and dramatic tensions, as Lorin Maazel has pointed out (see below), are given their due. The work may be a flawed masterpiece, a shade too ambitious for its own good, but masterpiece it seems to be in the hands and voices of Simon Rattle and his singers. This is a recreation of their Glyndebourne success of 1986, when the work took the house by storm. Later, concert performances were given with the same cast and at the same time it was recorded in the studio.

Rattle seems to revel in the buoyant rhythms, sensuous melodies and vivid orchestration in which Gershwin's score abounds, and even more importantly he conveys the sense of an evening in the theatre. Vocally the set is also a winner. Blackwell's glorious 'Summertime' is beguiling. Haymon is a soft-grained, moving Bess; Willard White a strong, sincere Porgy, perhaps the best there has ever been. Damon Evans is a spirited, amusing Sportin' Life; Gregg Baker a saturnine, commanding Crown. Smaller roles are taken with equal conviction, and the recording lives up, for the most part, to the calibre of the interpretation.

Recommended alternatives: Lorin Maazel (Decca) – this 1976 performance is even more disciplined, slightly less spontaneous than the Rattle with a cast that is virtually on a par with EMI's. It is headed by Leona Mitchell and Willard White (again) as the eponymous heroine and hero, with Barbara Hendricks as a pure-voiced Clara. It benefits from the playing and singing of the splendid Cleveland Orchestra and Chorus of which Maazel was then in charge. Skitch Henderson (RCA – excerpts only) – this disc preserves the memorable Bess of Leontyne Price in her prime in 1963, when she recorded these extracts. William Warfield is a resonant Porgy, John W. Bubbles a brilliant Sportin' Life. (Although not an opera the musical *Girl Crazy* (Elektra-Nonesuch) is a winner in this much-praised reconstruction of the original score.)

Kurt Weill (1900–50)

Die Dreigroschenoper (The Threepenny Opera). Ute Lemper (Polly), Milva (Jenny), Susanne Tremper (Lucy Brown), Helga Dernesch (Frau Peachum), René Kollo (Macheath), Mario Adorf (Peachum), Rolf Boysen (Street Singer), Berlin Radio Chamber Ch, Berlin Radio Sinfonietta/John Mauceri. (Decca 430 075-2)

The Threepenny Opera is a satire written by Weill in partnership with the playwright Bertolt Brecht, modelled on the eighteenth-century *Beggar's Opera*. The numbers, in dance rhythm and with orchestration that is jazz oriented while being uniquely Weill's in flavour, aptly capture the frank, easy-going, sleazy world of post-first-world-war Berlin. (It was first presented there in 1928.) Its most famous number is 'Mack the Knife', since distorted into all sorts of popular forms, but all the hard-hitting texts are matched by catchy tunes and curiously unsettling instrumentation. Its bitter irony, directed at the corrupt capitalism of the time, caused a sensation in Germany; so did the occasional mockery of conventional opera. Like all great composers, Weill created a sound world quite his own: it is notable for luminous textures, shifting harmonies, and insistent rhythms. Above all it is, as Rodney Milnes described it in *Opera on Record 3* (Hutchinson, 1984), 'subversion via comedy' – and that comedy must play a part in any production, as it does in the set listed here.

In recent times attempts have been made to revive the score as Weill intended it to be performed. This Decca version, virtually complete (including 'The Ballad of Sexual Dependency', cut before the first night), was part of this movement but unfortunately, for all its virtues, the role of Jenny, sung by a *diseuse*, isn't given at score pitch. On the other hand, Ute Lemper restores Polly to something like her original form and Kollo takes Macheath's music as written. Above all, Mauceri has soaked himself in the score and comes up with the authentic sound, helped by his Berlin forces and the excellent quality of the recording.

Recommended alternative: Wilhelm Brückner-Rüggeberg (CBS) – this admirable 1952 version, with a reasonably full text, has Lotte Lenya, the composer's widow, singing Jenny, the role she created. However by the time of this recording she transposed much of the music down, often an octave, sounding like a growling contralto and setting a bad precedent for her successors. To hear her in the original, turn to an excellent two-CD Teldec issue that has the first cast recorded in some numbers in 1930. This set also includes much else that wonderfully evokes that unrepeatable era in German art.

Street Scene. 1. Josephine Barstow (Mrs Maurrant), Angelina Réaux (Rose Maurrant), Meriel Dickinson (Mrs Jones),

Jerry Hadley (Sam Kaplan), David Kuebler (Mr Buchanan), Anthony Mee (Mr Fiorentino), Samuel Ramey (Frank Maurrant), Ch and O of Scottish Opera/John Mauceri. (Decca 433 371-2)

2. Kristine Ciesinski (Mrs Maurrant), Janis Kelly (Rose Maurrant), Meriel Dickinson (Mrs Jones), Bonaventura Bottone (Sam Kaplan), Harry Nicoll (Mr Buchanan), Peter Bronder (Mr Fiorentino), Richard Van Allan (Frank Maurrant), Ch and O of English National Opera/Carl Davis. (TER CDTER2 1185)

This interesting work dates from the composer's period as an emigré in the United States. 'Not until *Street Scene* did I achieve a real blending of drama and music', Weill averred at the time of the première in 1947. It is a setting of a play by Elmer Rice, who wrote the libretto, with lyrics by the left-wing writer Langston Hughes, and tells of a tragedy among the downtrodden inhabitants of New York tenements. It wonderfully combines humour, satire and romantic yearnings for better things. Musically Weill's skills from his German period are melded with what he learnt from American musicals and opera, but in no way is the work derivative: it speaks in its own individual tone. It deserves to rank with the best of Gershwin and Bernstein as representatives of a peculiarly American kind of opera. The score skilfully blends aria, *arioso*, *melodram* (speaking over music) and dialogue.

After being more or less ignored by record companies since its inception, two versions appeared in 1991. The Decca version is more strongly cast in the sense that it employs a fine cast of opera singers, mostly American, under Mauceri's alert direction, but the TER using the cast of the English National Opera performances has greater veracity. In particular, Ciesinski and Kelly convey indelibly, as they did on stage, their personal tragedies. On the other hand Ramey is probably preferable to Van Allan as Frank Maurrant, more authentically 'New York'. In both versions the moving quality of the score and its musical strengths are projected.

Michael Tippett (b. 1905)

King Priam. Heather Harper (Hecuba), Felicity Palmer (Andromache), Yvonne Minton (Helen), Philip Langridge (Paris), Robert Tear (Achilles), Kenneth Bowen (Hermes), Thomas Allen (Hector), Stephen Roberts (Patroclus), Norman Bailey (Priam), London Sinfonietta Ch, London Sinfonietta/David Atherton. (Decca 414 241-2)

Tippett's highly individual and frequently changing style has often kept him a step or two in advance of his audiences, so that they come to terms with his operas, as with his other sources, when he has moved on to new pastures. This has been particularly true of his operas in that he composes them to his own often abstruse and/or complex librettos. At one time *The Midsummer Marriage* (recorded by Philips with Colin Davis conducting and long awaited on CD) was considered 'difficult', but it has now been accepted as a potent allegory of spiritual and emotional growth and encompasses Tippett's favourite theme of the conflict between the dark and light sides of people's characters. His third opera, *The Knot Garden* (again Philips' marvellous recording, also under Colin Davis' direction, is badly wanted on CD), deals with the psychological side of the relationships between the principals depicted in a symbolic maze. Both scores are apt for their subjects and subtly crafted.

King Priam, Tippett's second opera, was thought spare, tough and inaccessible when first presented. Its depiction of the events of the Trojan war is used to discuss the subject of 'the mysterious nature of human choice' (Tippett). At the same time it is a pacifist's plea against the horrors, stupidity and inconsequence of war which is as relevant today as it was when the work was first performed in 1962. The plot is sharply dramatic with Achilles' war cry at the end of Act 1 as its exciting centre, but it also includes passages of lyrical beauty equivalent to those in *The Midsummer Marriage*. As a whole the score has an immediacy of impact and a stark reality which suggests it is the masterpiece among Tippett's operas. In spite of the tragedy expressed in the piece, one comes away from it, as from a great play, uplifted in spirit and more aware of the human predicament.

The work receives the recording it deserves under Atherton's sympathetic and alert direction. All difficulties disappear and his cast respond triumphantly to the composer's considerable challenges to their vocal technique. Similarly the admirable Sinfonietta cope easily with the instrumental difficulties. Bailey's moving Priam, Harper's tense Hecuba, Langridge's lyrical Paris and Tear's strong Achilles are all superb.

The Ice Break, Tippett's fourth opera, has just appeared on CD (Virgin Classics). It hardly achieves the level of inspiration of its predecessors. His most recent stage work, *New Year*, has been produced on television and will no doubt eventually appear on disc.

Dmitry Shostakovich (1906-75)

Lady Macbeth of the Mtsensk District. Galina Vishnevskaya (Katerina Ismailova), Birgit Finnilä (Sonyetka), Nicolai Gedda (Sergey), Werner Krenn (Zinovy Ismailov), Dimiter Petkov (Boris Ismailov), Ambrosian Opera Ch, London Philharmonic O/Mstislav Rostropovich. (EMI CDS7 49955-2)

Shostakovich's most significant opera was first given in 1934, then revised as *Katerina Ismailova* in 1963. Katerina, a rich merchant's wife starved of sex, is possessed with a desire for an erotic relationship, and chooses the handsome labourer Sergey. When her father-in-law Boris gets to know of the affair, he cruelly flogs Sergey. Katerina poisons the old man, and then when her husband discovers this she and Sergey murder him too. At their wedding their perfidy is revealed by the discovery of the husband's body and the pair are exiled as convicts to Siberia where Sergey, bored with Katerina, admires the flirtatious Sonyetka. Katerina pushes her in the river and jumps in after her.

A piece of stunning *verismo* Russian-style, it is indeed gratuitously violent, but the shock of the plot is tempered by Shostakovich's obvious sympathy for his anti-heroine on whom he lavished music of deep expressiveness. Her very obsession with love seems to exclude her feelings of morality, yet her tragedy, as she becomes haunted by her victims (like the original Lady Macbeth), provides material for a psychological study that the composer fully exploits. The revised version, not used here, toned down the blatant description of sexual activity and the satire of the police, which was apparently disliked by Stalin. However, the first version is the one to hear, especially when executed with such conviction as here by the composer's friends, Vishnevskaya and Rostropovich (wife and husband). He brings out all the frenzy and dissonance in the score while she draws from the title role every ounce of passion by virtue of her emotional powers. Gedda is just as convincing as the swaggering sensual Sergey.

Gian Carlo Menotti (b. 1911)

Amahl and the Night Visitors. James Rainbird (Amahl), Lorna Haywood (Mother), John Dobson (Kaspar), Donald Maxwell (Melchior), Curtis Watson (Balthazar), Ch and O of the Royal Opera House, Covent Garden/David Syrus. (TER CDTER 1124)

Menotti, an American of Italian origin, whose festivals at Spoleto in Italy and in Charleston USA, have promulgated his own and other composers' music over the years, is a conservatively minded musician who believes in writing easily assimilated score in readily accessible language. (He writes his own librettos.) He has composed successful operas on themes concerning modern life, the most famous being *The Consul*, a drama about political suppression in an unknown land that is as valid today as when it first appeared in 1950. After its immense success, he wrote a number of works, some of which achieved fame, but his star quickly waned, and *Amahl* is at present his only representation in the CD catalogue. It is a Christmas story that has maintained its popularity through its frequent appearance on television. This recording was made at the same time as stage performances in London and is a very fair representation of a charming if slightly sentimental tale. Lorna Haywood is particularly effective as the mother of the crippled Amahl who is cured by a miracle. The recording is excellent.

Benjamin Britten (1913–76)

Peter Grimes. 1. Claire Watson (Ellen Orford), Lauris Elms (Mrs Sedley), Jean Watson (Auntie), Peter Pears (Peter Grimes), Raymond Nilsson (Bob Boles), John Lanigan (Rector), Geraint Evans (Ned Keene), James Pease (Balstrode), Owen Brannigan (Swallow), David Kelly (Hobson), Ch and O of the Royal Opera House, Covent Garden/ Benjamin Britten. (Decca 414 577-2)

2. Heather Harper (Ellen Orford), Patricia Payne (Mrs Sedley), Elizabeth Bainbridge (Auntie), Jon Vickers (Peter Grimes), John Dobson (Bob Boles), John Lanigan (Rector), Thomas Allen (Ned Keene), Jonathan Summers (Balstrode), Forbes Robinson (Swallow), Richard Van Allan (Hobson), Ch and O of the Royal Opera House, Covent Garden/Colin Davis. (Philips 432 367-2)

Peter Grimes was inspired by an article by E.M. Forster (read by Britten in 1941, when he was in the USA) on the subject of the Suffolk poet George Crabbe. The libretto was fashioned by Montagu Slater from Crabbe's long poem, *The Borough*, the scene being Aldeburgh where Crabbe was born and bred and where Britten was to make his home shortly after writing this work. Its première at Sadler's Wells in 1945 made Britten's name and began the renaissance of British opera. Its anti-hero is the rough, independent, self-willed but poetic fisherman Grimes, the first of many outsiders depicted in Britten's operas. He is seen in conflict with the small-minded and prejudiced inhabitants of the Borough. The composer depicted them and Grimes unerringly within the context of a sea-drenched score which shows unflagging energy and inspiration. Britten's gift for drama, his uncanny sense of timing and his subtlety of characterisation all came of age at once.

The work's first recording is a historic document, conducted with natural authority by the composer and with Peter Pears, who created the part, as Grimes. His intense, moving and musical performance manages to catch the essence of the character. Even though Vickers, on the equally compelling Philips version, is more adept at suggesting the brusque, earthy nature of the character, he lacks Pears's musical accuracy and natural phrasing. Vickers makes Grimes into a tortured object of derision, more unhinged from the start. The portrayals are complementary. Davis's reading is more extreme than Britten's, using both slower and faster tempi and the orchestral colours seem darker, more opaque. Davis makes one realise that Britten is the true inheritor of the mantle of Verdi and Tchaikovsky, two composers Britten deeply admired. But, of course, Britten's own reading bears the stamp of a creator's authority.

The orchestral playing is admirable on both sets; the choral singing has more bite on the Davis. Both sets employed singers who were familiar with their roles from performances at Covent Garden. Claire Watson sings Ellen's part more beautifully than Harper, but Harper has the deeper insight into the character. Pease is the more mature, therefore more relevant Balstrode. On the whole the Decca recording (by Erik Smith) is to be preferred, being clearer in detail and attempting to simulate a stage performance as the Philips does not.

As a pendant to these versions it will be worth acquiring the amazingly vivid extracts recorded in 1948 (EMI) when they appear on CD, with the unsurpassed Ellen of Joan Cross (the creator) and the younger Pears unbearably moving in Grimes's mad scene. Goodall, who conducted the première, is in charge here.

The Rape of Lucretia. Heather Harper (Female Chorus), Jenny Hill (Lucia), Janet Baker (Lucretia), Elizabeth Bainbridge (Bianca), Peter Pears (Male Chorus), Benjamin Luxon (Tarquinius), Bryan Drake (Junius), John Shirley-Quirk (Collatinus), English Chamber O/Benjamin Britten. (Decca 425 666-2)

Britten's first chamber opera (première at Glyndebourne, 1946), using the small forces of his own English Opera Group, is one of the tautest, most compelling and eloquent scores he ever penned, with an unjustly vilified libretto by poet Ronald Duncan. The two acts, which are each divided into two scenes, depict the ravishing of the pure Lucretia by Tarquinius (the result of a challenge from his military colleagues) in or near Rome in 500 BC, within a musical and dramatic frame provided by the dispassionate Female and Male Chorus, who declaim a Christian message. The moving marriage of Lucretia and Collatinus is torn apart by the rape, and she commits suicide, unable to bear the shame.

Britten created the title role for Kathleen Ferrier (non-commercial discs preserve parts of a live performance with her). Janet Baker was Ferrier's natural successor, and she sings the part with the heart-rending dignity and beauty it demands, nowhere more so than in her morning-after solo. Shirley-Quirk makes much of little as the faithful, noble Collatinus. Luxon is properly priapic as the rude Tarquinius. The set is completed by Baker's account of Britten's *Phaedra*, a dramatic cantata written for her, and one of the composer's late masterpieces.

There exist substantial extracts of one of the original casts of *Lucretia* featuring Nancy Evans (who alternated with Ferrier in the early performances) as a moving Lucretia. These have yet to appear on CD.

Albert Herring. Sylvia Fisher (Lady Billows), April Cantelo (Miss Wordsworth), Catherine Wilson (Nancy), Johanna Peters (Florence Pike), Sheila Rex (Mrs Herring), Peter Pears (Albert Herring), Edgar Evans (Mr Upfold), Joseph Ward (Sid), Owen Brannigan (Budd), John Noble (Mr Gedge), English Chamber O/Benjamin Britten. (Decca 421 849-2)

This delightful comedy, another chamber opera, followed a year after *Lucretia*, when it was also given at Glyndebourne. Based on a short story by Guy de Maupassant, Eric Crozier's libretto transfers the action from France to East Anglia. It tells how the worthies of the imaginary Suffolk village of Loxford, unable to find a virginal May Queen, choose instead a virginal May King – Albert – who, after getting drunk at the celebrations enthroning him, goes off on a binge, taking in wine, women and song. Britten's gift for acute satire and sharp-edged characterisation comes into its own in this finely honed and astute comedy, which won new friends when presented at Glyndebourne in the 1980s.

This performance, recorded in 1964, uses singers from the English Opera Group who were familiar with their roles from performances on stage. The cast is headed by Pears, the original Albert, who shows a nice vein of comedy. Fisher is a dominating and domineering Lady Billows. Both the singing and the playing simulate the enjoyment of a stage account, and Britten conducts with his customary alertness. Altogether this well-recorded performance promises many hours of quiet pleasure. Tapes exist of the original cast; one day they may be transferred to CD.

Billy Budd. Peter Pears (Captain Vere), Gregory Dempsey (Red Whiskers), Robert Tear (Novice), Peter Glossop (Billy Budd), John Shirley-Quirk (Mr Redburn), Bryan Drake (Mr Flint), Owen Brannigan (Dansker), Michael Langdon (Claggart), Wandsworth School Boys' Choir, Ambrosian Opera Ch, London Symphony O/Benjamin Britten. (Decca 417 428-2)

Britten's second large-scale opera was first given at Covent Garden in 1951, conducted by the composer. The libretto, by E.M. Forster and Eric Crozier, is based on a story by Herman Melville. The outcast here is the handsome eager Billy Budd, whose sole flaw, his stammer, causes his downfall when he cannot reply to false accusations by the master-at-arms Claggart. In his frustration, Billy strikes his accuser dead in front of a court martial, headed by the good Captain Vere, who could save Billy but fails to do so. The hidden context here is the stifled homosexual desires of Claggart, and presumably Vere, although at the time of the première these could not, of course, be overtly stated. But no such reticence hinders the depiction of the brutality and poor conditions in the Navy in 1797, just after the mutinies at Spithead and the Nore: these recent memories are another reason why Budd, as a possible catalyst for mutiny, has to be sacrificed. Britten conveys all these strands in masterly fashion both in his score and in his own reading of it, dating from 1967. The superb cast is headed by Pears as an appropriately equivocal, sensitive Vere (whose memories, as an old man, of the unhappy events frame the action), Peter Glossop as a virile, open-hearted Billy and Michael Langdon as a saturnine Claggart.

The Turn of the Screw. David Hemmings (Miles), Olive Dyer (Flora), Jennifer Vyvyan (Governess), Arda Mandikian (Miss Jessel), Joan Cross (Mrs Grose), Peter Pears (Peter Quint), English Opera Group O/Benjamin Britten. (Decca 425 672-2 (mono))

This chamber opera, to a libretto by Myfanwy Piper based on Henry James's short story of the same name, was first presented at Venice in 1954 with the cast of this recording. It is often considered Britten's masterpiece in the genre, so taut and consistent is the writing, so mesmeric its effect in any half-tolerable performance. This is a great one, catching completely the equivocal, mysterious nature of both story and opera. Britten's unerring evocation of Bly (a country house) and his depiction of the nervous, overwrought Governess, the seemingly corrupted children and the ghosts are conveyed in a confident, secure reading under the composer's watchful eye. Nobody to date has bettered Vyvyan vocally or dramatically as the Governess. Few have equalled the other singers, all at ease in their parts and perfectly cast. Hemmings's defiant Miles, Pears's chilling, insidious Quint, Joan Cross's endearing Mrs Grose (her final role) are just the best of an excellent group. This is at once a historic document and a riveting experience.

A Midsummer Night's Dream. Elizabeth Harwood (Titania), Heather Harper (Helena), Josephine Veasey (Hermia), Helen Watts (Hippolyta), Alfred Deller (Oberon), Peter Pears (Lysander), Thomas Hemsley (Demetrius), John Shirley-Quirk (Theseus), Owen Brannigan (Bottom), Norman Lumsden (Quince), Choirs of Downside and Emmanuel Schools, London Symphony O/Benjamin Britten. (Decca 425 663-2)

Peter Pears himself deftly reduced Shakespeare's long play to a libretto of manageable length, losing very little that is essential. The piece was first given in the Jubilee Hall at Aldeburgh in 1960 with Britten in charge, then presented at Covent Garden later that year, when Solti was the conductor. The score is a miracle of lightness and delicacy, evoking ideally the various, dream-like aspects of the story, most successfully of all in the scenes for Titania and Oberon. Magical too are the beginning, which suggests the awakening in the wood, and the close, an address, in speech, from Puck. This recording was made, with several of the roles' creators. Among them is Deller, the original Oberon, whose ethereal assumption of the part is sung with true other-worldly tone and profile, though later interpreters have given it a more threatening aspect. Harwood is a lovely and fluent Titania, Brannigan, the first Bottom, is vital and amusing. The 1966 recording wears its years lightly.

Curlew River. Peter Pears (Madwoman), John Shirley-Quirk (Ferryman), Bryan Drake (Traveller), Harold Blackburn (Abbot), English Opera Group/Benjamin Britten and Viola Tunnard. (Decca 421 858-2)

This was the first and most compelling of Britten's three 'parables for church performance' written in the 1960s. Its inspiration was a Japanese Noh drama (seen by Britten on a visit to Japan), reset by the composer and librettist William Plomer in the fenlands of East Anglia as a mediaeval Christian mystery play. It tells of a madwoman who seeks to cross the Curlew River to find the son stolen from her. Instead she encounters his spirit who gives her his blessing. Britten's highly original, spare writing once again shows him breaking new ground and finding precisely the right idiom for the work in hand. In the tradition of the Noh dramas, the cast is all male. Pears sings the Madwoman with sincerity and urgency, splendidly supported by Shirley-Quirk's strong Ferryman. The playing of the seven instrumentalists is beyond praise. The recording was made in Orford Parish Church, where the work was first given in 1964. Its slightly less inspired successors, *The Burning Fiery Furnace* and *The Prodigal Son*, are also on Decca CDs.

Death in Venice. Peter Pears (Aschenbach), James Bowman (Voice of Apollo), John Shirley-Quirk (seven roles), English Opera Group Ch, English Chamber O/Steuart Bedford. (Decca 425 669-2)

Britten wrote this, his last opera, when suffering from the heart complaint that eventually killed him. Though composed under stress, it shows little diminution in his powers. He was determined to finish it as a final gift to his lifelong friend, Peter Pears, who has the long and taxing role of Aschenbach in Myfanwy Piper's libretto based on Thomas Mann's novella. He dispatches it with all the vocal and verbal command for which he was famous. He catches all the dilemma of the man of letters drawn irrevocably

toward the call of Dionysus as represented by the Polish boy (a
dancing part), itself containing autobiographical elements on
Britten's side. As the ephemeral characters flitting in and out of
Aschenbach's consciousness, Shirley-Quirk gives a virtuoso performance. Bedford, Britten's faithful disciple, who took over the
1973 première when Britten was too ill to conduct it, is the wholly
committed and convincing interpreter of Britten's wishes. The
recording is faultless.

> *Paul Bunyan.* Elisabeth Comeaux Nelson (Tiny), Pop Wagner
> (Narrator), James Lawless (Paul Bunyan – speaking role),
> Dan Dressen (Johnny Inkslinger), James Bohn (Hel Helson),
> Plymouth Music Series Ch and O/Philip Brunelle. (Virgin
> Classics VCD7 90710-2)

This was Britten's first opera, written to a libretto by W.H. Auden
when both artists were in the USA during the war, but later
suppressed by the composer. Its recent revival shows this quasi-
musical to be enormous fun, imbued with Auden's verbal high
jinks and Britten's musical wit. It was revised by Britten in 1974
when it was performed successfully on the radio. This 1988
recording, made at the time of live performances given at the
Maltings, Snape, is thoroughly authentic in presenting the story
of the mythical folk-hero of the title, evoking unerringly its odd
combination of folksiness and sophistication under the alert baton
of Brunelle. Accents are genuinely American.

Leonard Bernstein (1918–90)

> *Candide.* June Anderson (Cunegonde), Christa Ludwig (Old
> Lady), Jerry Hadley (Candide), Nicolai Gedda (Governor,
> Vanderdendur, Ragotski), Adolph Green (Dr Pangloss,
> Martin), London Symphony Ch and O/Leonard Bernstein.
> (DG 419 734-2, also on video, laserdisc)

Bernstein was instrumental in bridging the gap between opera
and this century's popular music with his catchy tunes, infectious
rhythms, and off-centre harmonies. Nowhere was the liaison
more manifest than in this daring score – opera, operetta, musical,

satire all rolled into one. However, it has never enjoyed an unmitigated success on stage: Bernstein's literature-based work (Voltaire) has never enjoyed the earthy, direct appeal of the genuine musical *West Side Story* (available on another DG issue conducted by the composer with opera stars Te Kanawa and Carreras in the main roles). In consequence it has undergone all sorts of changes under different hands in its chequered history. In 1980 John Mauceri directed a production for Scottish Opera that attempted to come as close as possible to realising the score as a true entity with many cuts restored. The production proved the piece stageworthy and was the spur for this excellent recording conducted by the composer on his last London appearance.

The reinstated music includes what Bernstein termed his 'Puccini aria', 'Nothing more than this', Candide's expression of disillusionment near the end of the work. It proves well worth the rescue act, especially as Hadley is the best member of a cast consisting mostly of opera singers, not all completely happy in the genre. One recruit from the world of the musical is the veteran Adolph Green as the many-faceted, tongue-twisting Pangloss. He has little voice to speak of, but knows his way round a wordy lyric. Bernstein conducts everything with panache and love, the self-admiration sometimes leading him into over-deliberate tempi that hold up the action. The LSO plays superbly for him, giving the score a grandeur that Bernstein may have imagined only in his wildest dreams. Is it all a bit over the top? If so, there are many who will obviously like it that way. And Bernstein is undoubtedly a towering figure in the music-drama of the second half of this century.

Harrison Birtwistle (b. 1934)

Punch and Judy. Jan De Gaetani (Judy, Fortune Teller), Phyllis Bryn-Julson (Pretty Polly, Witch), Philip Langridge (Lawyer), Stephen Roberts (Punch), David Wilson-Johnson (Choregos, Jack Ketch), John Tomlinson (Doctor), London Sinfonietta/David Atherton. (Etcetera KTC 2014)

Birtwistle has always shown an aptitude for the stage. This chamber piece, written before the composer's grander operas (which are regrettably unrecorded), is a black comedy based by librettist Stephen Pruslin on the Punch and Judy story. When first given at Aldeburgh in 1968 it is said to have shocked Britten into leaving his own theatre. It includes much gratuitous violence from the amoral Punch, fiercely delineated by Birtwistle's score, but also moments of poignant beauty. It is written in one long, unremittingly tense act, creating a hypnotic effect on stage and on disc. In this wholly admirable recording, Atherton, who directed the première, conducts a taut, accurate and exciting performance of this somewhat sinister piece with its mythic overtones. The cast is uniformly superb. At home one has the advantage of following and comprehending Pruslin's brilliant libretto with its many verbal conceits. The recording is vivid. Recommended to the enterprising.

COLLECTIONS AND RECITALS

The early history of recording was almost exclusively concerned with singers, whose voices were reproduced with reasonable faithfulness by the old horn. Fortuitously the first years of the century were also notable for a plethora of great singers. Their performances give us an insight into the operatic style of bygone years, stretching back into Victorian times. They are historic documents of some value.

In the following decades singers of later generations continued to record prolifically – for instance the German soprano Lotte Lehmann (see below) cut literally hundreds of double-sided 78rpm discs throughout her career, from 1918 to her retirement in 1951. These originals were a profitable source of reissue in the LP era. Now in the CD era, with greatly improved technical facilities, these old records can be lovingly refurbished; indeed they are perhaps heard with more fidelity than at any time in their history. In the era of LP, yet another generation of singers made memorable discs, this time recitals of some fifty minutes' length. Many of the best of these are now being reissued on CD, while artists of today also make solo discs. Inevitably a choice from this wealth of material will be personal and arbitrary, but the CDs listed below should give an enthusiast a taste of the width and variety of choice available – and, of course, a rewarding treasury of gorgeous singing. Many more are to be found on the important reissue labels – EMI, Pearl, Preiser and Nimbus (although the discs of the last-named must be treated with some caution, as it adds resonance to the originals).

Covent Garden on Record: a history: Vol 1 (1874–1904) and *Vol. 2 (1904–1910).* (Pearl GEMM CDS 9923-4) (each Vol. has three CDs)

This is the first half of a huge project relating the history in sound of the Royal Opera House from around 1870 to 1940. Its mentor is Keith Hardwick, former guru of the archives at EMI and so responsible for 'The Record of Singing' and for many of the reissues of individual singers listed below. Now a freelance, he makes the most of his knowledge and his vast collection of 78rpm records. This commendable project is a satisfying and painless way for any inquiring and/or young collector to become acquainted with a whole host of artists from the so-called Golden Age of Singing. Although the earliest recording in the first volume dates from 1903, several of the singers included, such as the legendary Adelina Patti (born as long ago as 1843 and consenting to make records in her Welsh retreat at the age of 61), and Tamagno and Maurel (respectively the first Otello and Iago) were active in the 1870s and '80s. So were the great French baritone Lassalle (b.1847), the noble bass Edouard de Reszke (b. 1853, recorded 1903), and the grand soprano Lilli Lehmann (b. 1848, who made a succession of discs in her sixties showing her to have lost little or none of her voice or technique). These figures from the dawn of recording history are followed by a group that helped establish the gramophone, among them, the Australian prima donna, Melba, De Lucia (a tenor of extraordinary calibre and sensitivity), the noted French soprano Calvé (who lived on to 1942), the delightful bass, Pol Plançon, and the massive-voiced baritone Titta Ruffo. All are worthily represented in Volume 1.

Volume 2 includes singers who were in their prime during the century's first decade, headed by Caruso (see also below) and such astonishing singers as Tetrazzini, McCormack (regrettably under-represented at present elsewhere on CD), Giuseppe De Luca (aristocrat among baritones), the stentorian tenor, Giovanni Zenatello (Tamagno's successor as Otello), the sovereign baritone Pasquale Amato, his lighter, more brilliant senior Battistini and many, many others. The second pair of volumes should be available shortly.

The Record of Singing, Volume 4: From 1939 to the End of the 78 Era.
(EMI CHS7 69741 2) (seven CDs)

This is the fourth and last volume of a huge project covering the history of singing on disc during the first half of this century. The four volumes appeared over the past decade on LP and so far only Volume 4 has been transferred to CD with a number of extra singers. This final period of the 78rpm era was rich in both singers and repertory. It saw the distinguished autumn of a number of artists who had made the substantial part of their careers before the Second World War and the engrossing spring of others who would go on to greater things in the LP era. In that respect the period may be regarded as transitional; yet the actual achievement recorded on these discs is of absorbing interest in its own right. The security of technique of bygone days (those covered on the Covent Garden issue above) is often combined with a more searching approach to interpretation. The volume also records in another sense the end of a period which had existed for decades in which singers were part of regular ensembles. For better, but probably for worse, that is now a thing of the past. In those days singers tended to specialise in one *Fach* (type of repertory) and/or opera in their own language.

The volume is categorised by countries and schools in this order: Anglo-American, French, German, Scandinavian, Russian and Slavonic, Italian. It includes such famous names as Callas (who actually ends the whole project with a magnificent live account of the finale of Rossini's *Armida* recorded in 1954 in San Remo), Flagstad, Milanov, Jurinac, Schwarzkopf, Seefried, Ferrier, de los Angeles, Schock, Gedda, Hotter, Tebaldi, Simionato, and Christoff. They are all represented by choice items, but it also includes names that are unfamiliar even to *cognoscenti* of the period. The set is a veritable cornucopia of magnificent singing and interpretation: at once varied, illuminating, thrilling. Nobody who cares about the history of operatic interpretation should be without it.

'Les Introuvables du Chant Mozartien'. Various singers (EMI CMS7 63750-2) (four discs)

This collection of performances of excerpts from Mozart's operas, mostly from the first half of the century, contains many famous and several rare recordings. In Mozart, it can be argued that the present age is at least the equal of its predecessor. Certainly styles have changed radically, yet there is much to be learnt here in terms of a vocal beauty seldom encountered today and particularly an unrivalled sense of *legato*. In all it is a fascinating history of how Mozart has been interpreted during the period of recording.

'Les Italiens à Paris'. Arias by Spontini, Donizetti, Verdi, Salieri. Various singers. (Chant du Monde LDC 278 898)

A fascinating disc that includes arias written by Italian composers for Paris. Usually heard in Italian translation, they are all performed here in the original French by native French singers. Particularly interesting are the pieces from Donizetti's *La favorite* and Verdi's *Les vêpres Siciliennes*.

Operatic finales: R. Strauss: **Salome**; Cherubini: **Medée**; Janáček: **The Makropolos Affair**; Puccini (completed Alfano): **Turandot**. Josephine Barstow, Scottish Opera Ch and O/John Mauceri. (Decca 430 203-2)

This issue is remarkable for two reasons. Firstly, it is the best representation of the intense, intelligent art of a notable British soprano, whose career, mainly with the English National Opera, has been a distinguished one ranging over a wide span of the repertory. Secondly, the disc includes the first uncut recording of Alfano's completion of Puccini's *Turandot*. It proves a far more satisfying conclusion to Puccini's last score than that customarily heard in the theatre. Barstow is impressive here in a role that she hasn't yet attempted on stage. She is even better suited by the Strauss and Janáček where her complete identification with two very different anti-heroines, both of whom she has portrayed in the opera house, is astonishing and thrilling. To that she adds the closing scene of Cherubini's work, seldom heard in its original French (rather than Italian) version. These vivid assumptions are eagerly supported by Mauceri and his orchestra.

Cecilia Bartoli sings Rossini Arias. (Decca 425 430-2)

Bartoli is by far the youngest singer represented in this section, but she deserves her place among the great for her keen accomplishment, already acknowledged, in Rossini. She has both the voice and technique to master the line and runs of arias from *L'Italiana in Algeri, Cenerentola, Tancredi, La donna del lago*, and *La pietra del paragone*; then shows the delicacy and pathos needed for Desdemona's Willow Song from *Otello*, the model for Verdi's later setting. Here is high promise indeed (try also a further selection of

Rossini (Decca 436 075-2) and *Cecilia Bartoli sings Mozart Arias*, (Decca 430 513-2)

Carlo Bergonzi – 31 Tenor Arias by Verdi. New Philharmonic O/ Nello Santi and Royal Philharmonic O/Lamberto Gardelli. (Philips 432 486-2)

This comprehensive set (three CDs), recorded in 1975, includes practically every Verdi aria from his first opera, *Oberto*, to his last, *Falstaff*. They are sung by the leading Verdi stylist among tenors in the post-war era. In a period dominated by the famous Three Tenors (Pavarotti, Domingo and Carreras), it is easy to forget their immediate predecessor, whose sovereign line and steady, easily produced tone was such a feature of performances of Verdi's works around the world from the mid-'50s to the late '80s, a period during which he maintained his control of voice and style almost unsullied by the passing years. When he made this collection, he may have been past his absolute prime, but his singing remains as refined and musical as ever.

***Victoria de los Angeles – Early Recordings*:** Arias by Verdi, Puccini, Boito, Rossini, Mascagni, Catalani, Wagner, Mozart, Gounod. (EMI CDH7 63495-2)

De los Angeles burst onto the opera scene after the war with her delightful personality and warm, appealing voice. She was soon in demand in all the international opera houses and in the recording studios. Her tone, rounded, true and vibrant, took naturally to recording, where the directness of her style could be palpably felt. Here in this music, much of which she never sang on stage, she shows off her art attractively, with some readings that have remained classics across the years, not least Elsa's Dream from *Lohengrin* and Desdemona's Willow Song and Ave Maria from Verdi's *Otello*.

Jussi Björling sings operatic arias. (EMI CDH7 61053-2)

Björling possessed a voice of peculiarly plangent beauty, which he used with an innate and unfailing sense of aristocratic style, never indulging in the occasional vulgarities of his Italian counterparts.

His career began in his native Sweden when he was still in his teens. After spreading his wings in Europe before the war, he established himself as the leading tenor at the Metropolitan in the Italian and French repertory from 1939 until his untimely death, aged 49, twenty years later. This CD derives from his 78 records made when he was in his absolute prime, before the war, including an account of 'Nessun dorma' that puts even Pavarotti's in the shade. As a supplement, try *Legendary Performers – Jussi Björling* (RCA RD 85934), made up of items recorded during the tenor's period in New York and a recital on Bluebell, a Swedish label (ABCD 006), which has some marvellous items recorded in Holland in 1939 and Norway in 1959.

Maria Callas: Mad Scenes and Bel Canto arias. (EMI CDC7 4783-2)
Maria Callas: Puccini and Bellini arias. (EMI CDC7 47966-2)

Callas is represented in the catalogue by a great number of reissues. Many are drawn from her complete sets, described above in the composer section of this book. These two, made in her prime, are drawn from LP recitals of repertory, some of which she did not again broach. The first includes the mad scenes from Donizetti's *Anna Bolena* (a notable Callas assumption at La Scala), Bellini's *Il pirata*, and Thomas's *Hamlet* plus extracts from three other Donizetti pieces, all showing off the famous diva's vocal and emotional gifts at their most striking. The other disc, apart from early and recommendable extracts from Bellini's *La Sonnambula*, comprises performances of arias by Puccini that have seldom been surpassed for their interpretative insights.

Carreras, Domingo and Pavarotti in concert. With O of Rome Opera/Zubin Mehta. (Decca 430 433-2) (also available on video/laserdisc).

The World Cup outdoor concert (at Rome's Caracalla Baths) that did so much to promote the cause of opera. All three tenors are in tremendous form.

The Complete Caruso. (Pearl EVC I–IV) (four volumes of three
CDs each)

It is truthfully said that Caruso made the gramophone and the
gramophone made Caruso. Various attempts have been made to
transfer to LP and CD the ancient 78s that enshrine the repertory
of the century's most famous tenor. By and large this huge
enterprise is the most successful (far preferable to those made by
RCA, descendant of the company which made the original
recordings – which should be avoided!). Pearl has remained
faithful to the originals, working with excellent copies and
eliminating only such noise as can be taken away without
affecting the voice. One soon becomes accustomed to the old-
fashioned sound and listens to the unique voice, an instrument
that resembles a Rolls Royce in the sense that the reserves of
power seem limitless. The tone itself is warm and velvety, akin to
a ripe Burgundy. By and large its owner uses it with a fine balance
of musicality, fervent communication and sheer enjoyment.

The recordings made between 1902 and 1920 disclose the
change in Caruso's voice from a lyrical, fresh, free tone to the
richer, darker, slightly more effortful sound of the later years.
Caruso ranged widely in Italian and French opera, recording arias
from most of his favourite roles, some of them several times over.
Then there are the songs, where the great man relaxes into the
outpourings of love and the ditties that were virtually the pop
numbers of the day. In these Caruso is even more at home than
Pavarotti today. However here we are strictly concerned with
opera – and Caruso leaves us in no doubt that, in particular, his
Verdi and Puccini heroes were a thing apart, overwhelming in
their interpretative power. They will always stand the test of
time.

Enrico Caruso: Opera Arias and Songs – 1902–1904. (EMI CDH7
61046-2)

If you don't want the comprehensive collection above, you might
settle for this issue of Caruso's earliest recordings, captured by
recording pioneer Fred Gaisberg in Milan. They were made for
G&T, predecessor of HMV, before the tenor signed with Victor
in 1904. They have been finely refurbished here.

Chaliapin sings Russian Opera Arias. (EMI CDH7 61009-2)

Chaliapin, the great Russian bass, was one of the foremost opera singers and actors of the century. Trained in Imperial Russia under stringent circumstances, he learnt his art from the notable actors and producers of that time. In consequence the famed bass parts of Russian opera have seldom had such a convincing interpreter. Sometimes he could go too far in emotional effect, but most of the performances here, made when he was at the peak of his powers, are stunning – real characters leap off the disc.

Boris Christoff: Opera Arias. (EMI CDM7 69542)

Christoff was one of the major figures in the history of post-war opera. (He features on the front of the 'Record of Singing' box, see above.) He bestrode the stages of Europe with his strongly projected, resonant, Slavic voice, formidable presence and command of Italian and Russian. On this important reissue, he can be heard in most of his leading roles – Boris Godunov (his earliest and best recordings from Mussorgsky's opera), Prince Galitsky, Attila, Philip II, Fiesco (*Simon Boccanegra*, see also entry on Verdi), and Padre Guardiano among others. In all his incisive diction and well-modulated tone are impressive.

Laurence Dale. Arias from operas by Massenet, Boieldieu, Thomas, Lalo, Adam, Bizet, Messager, and Bazin. Nancy Symphony O/ Kenneth Montgomery. (Chant du Monde LDC 278 934)

The young British tenor Laurence Dale here undertakes to revive pieces from operas sadly neglected in recent times, and brings to their execution excellent French, idiomatic tone and a sure sense of the right style. He reminds us that works such as Massenet's *Grisélidis*, Adam's *Postillon de Lonjumeau* and Bazin's *Maître Pathelin* are worthy of revival.

Giuseppe di Stefano sings Opera Arias and Songs. (EMI CDM7 63105-2)

Di Stefano appeared on the opera scene immediately after the war and, with his bright, attractive tenor and ardent manner, immediately made his mark. In recordings he became Callas's regular partner. His career was foreshortened when he unwisely undertook roles too heavy for his lyric tenor. This disc preserves the best of his early recordings when his voice was in pristine condition, plus some extracts from his complete opera sets made a few years later. It shows why he was such a sought-after and appealing artist.

Placido Domingo and Katia Riccarelli: Verdi: Arias and Duets. (Decca 421 863-2)

This disc has these two much loved artists singing extracts from Verdi's operas with refined tone and appreciable understanding. Domingo is elsewhere represented by many recitals, most of them excerpted from his complete sets. *The Best of Domingo* (DG 427 708-2) and *Placido Domingo sings Opera Arias* (EMI CDM7 63103-2) are the most satisfying collections.

Nicolai Gedda - Opera Arias. (EMI CDM7 69550-2)

The Swedish tenor's career has stretched from 1952 to today during which he kept most of his vocal strength and technique intact. An excellent linguist, he is at home in Italian, French and Russian - as this recital derived from recordings made when he was at his best confirms. As Roméo, Benvenuto Cellini (in Berlioz's opera), Huon (Weber's *Oberon*), Lohengrin and Lensky (one of the most moving accounts of his aria from *Eugene Onegin* ever made) among others, he is unrivalled in the post-war age. His voice was basically lyrical, but strong enough to attempt parts that are often considered the province of more heroically inclined tenors. This is a fair and rewarding representation of Gedda's attractive art.

Beniamino Gigli: Operatic Arias. (EMI CDH7 61051-2)
Beniamino Gigli: Operatic Arias. (RCA GD 87811)

Gigli was the leading Italian lyric tenor in the era immediately following Caruso's hegemony. In Italy, then at the Metropolitan in New York, then again in Italy he established an enviable reputation. He had the most pure, beautiful Italian tenor of the century, bar none, and he possessed the vital gift of communication. In his day he was as popular as Pavarotti. Here he can be heard in some of the most popular arias ever penned, all sung with glorious tone and natural appeal, even if the style is sometimes a shade vulgar. The EMI issue ranges over his whole career; the RCA contains performances made in the 1920s when he was at the Met. and in his absolute prime, and includes duets with many of his most notable colleagues of the day.

Tito Gobbi: Opera Aria Recital. (EMI CDM7 63109-2)

Gobbi was one of the most noted actor-singers of the early post-war era. Possessor of an individual, pungent baritone, he used it with an acute feeling for the text and the meaning of the score in hand. This disc contains a number of his earliest, war-time recordings on 78 and extracts from some of his complete sets. Here samples of Rossini, Donizetti, Verdi and Puccini are enshrined which mark him out as an interpreter of the highest class, varying his tone and style to the needs of his roles.

Sena Jurinac – Opera and Song Recital. Arias by Mozart, Smetana, Tchaikovsky, and Strauss's 'Four Last Songs'. (EMI CDH7 63199-2)

Jurinac was one of the loveliest artists to appear after the war, becoming a leading light of the Vienna State Opera and Glyndebourne. She also sang regularly in Italy and at Covent Garden. Her voice had a heart-warming timbre and she used it with a total absence of artifice or sophistication. All the emotions are expressed with complete sincerity. Arias from *Idomeneo* and *Così fan tutte* will remind older listeners of her Glyndebourne appearances. As Lisa in *The Queen of Spades*, she sings with the correct fervent feelings. As a bonus there are the Strauss songs, a live performance of illuminating beauty.

Alexander Kipnis. (Preiser 89018)

This imposing Russian bass spent most of his career in Berlin and New York where his dark, resonant voice and powerful acting made him constantly in demand between the wars. Here we have the best of him on his HMV discs of the 1920s and '30s. Examples of his Mozart, Verdi and Gounod roles are supplemented by other choice items. All are sung with the same security and feeling.

Lotte Lehmann sings Operatic Arias. (EMI CDH7 61042-2)

Lehmann was star of the Vienna State Opera and just about every other opera house from her début in 1914 until around 1945. She had a lovely, warm soprano and an impulsive, spontaneous way of singing that conquered all hearts. Although she was equally at home in German, Italian and French repertory, her most famous parts were Leonore in *Fidelio*, which she sang for some ten years (1927-37) at the Salzburg Festival, latterly under Toscanini, and the Strauss heroines: she was an unrivalled Marschallin in *Der Rosenkavalier* (qv), Ariadne and Arabella. She made many recordings in the acoustic era and many more in the days of electrical recording on 78. Some of her most appealing portrayals are remembered here.

The Art of Frida Leider. (Preiser 89301) (three CDs)

The great German inter-war dramatic soprano was notable at Bayreuth and Covent Garden for her Wagner assumptions, but earlier in her career she was noted in Mozart, Verdi and much else. This comprehensive issue records in every way the grand yet soft-grained character of her glorious singing. Everything is sung in German, but who cares when all is executed with such supreme confidence? Souvenirs of her exemplary readings of Wagner, her earlier and better performances, are also included.

Giovanni Martinelli – Opera Recital. (Nimbus NI 7804)

Martinelli was Caruso's immediate successor at the Metropolitan, and his career there extended for thirty-three years, from 1913 to '46, during which time he was heard in a wide variety of parts. He was perhaps the greatest Verdi stylist of the century among tenors. His voice of a highly individual, slightly dry character, is an acquired taste – but once acquired the listener realises that here is an interpreter in a thousand. This CD comprises some of his most desirable recordings from the 1920s when he was in his prime.

Here enshrined are memories of his unique Manrico, Radames, Andrea Chénier, and Canio among others. This is a suitable pendant to his complete *Otello* recommended under the Verdi entry.

Melchior sings Wagner. (EMI CDH7 69789-2)

Lauritz Melchior, active in all the world's major houses from 1924 to 1946, was the greatest Wagnerian *Heldentenor* (i.e. heroic tenor) of the century, probably of all time. His voice had just the metal, ring, warmth and technical control to do full justice to Wagner's taxing music for his heroes. He also possessed another essential requirement in this music – seemingly endless stamina. On this invaluable disc many of his HMV recordings, made when he was in his prime during the late 1920s and '30s are preserved for posterity to wonder at. Here are the solos for Rienzi, Tannhäuser, Lohengrin, Walther, Tristan, Siegmund, and Siegfried sung with complete confidence and assurance. In two passages alone, Tannhäuser's Rome Narration and Tristan's appeal to Isolde to follow him at the end of Act 2, the sincerity and involvement of Melchior's interpretations are there for all to hear. So is the sheer exuberance of Siegfried's forging solos. (See also entry on Wagner.)

Zinka Milanov/Opera and Song Recital. (RCA GD 60074)

Milanov was the reigning soprano in the *spinto* repertory at the Metropolitan for thirty years from 1937. She possessed a lovely voice, capable of soaring easily above an orchestra and of the most refined *pianissimo*. This is a fair representation of her repertory including souvenirs of her Norma, *Trovatore* and *Forza del Destino* Leonoras, Amelia, Gioconda, and Santuzza. The disc also includes a beautiful account of Rusalka's Moon aria and some moving performances of songs. (See also entry on Verdi.)

Claudia Muzio sings Opera Arias and Songs. (EMI CDH7 69790-2)

Muzio, active from 1910 until her early death in 1936, was an Italian soprano with a surpassingly beautiful voice of individual character which she used with supreme intelligence to express deep emotions. In this respect she had only one equal this century – Maria Callas. Muzio was particularly notable as Verdi's Violetta and Desdemona. Many of her early recordings were made for minor companies in the period of acoustical recording. In the last years of her career, however, she made a series of invaluable recordings for Columbia, most of them included on this reissue, well remastered. They provide plentiful evidence of Muzio's ability to act with the voice and demonstrate her complete commitment to her repertory. By contrast note the lighter, flirtatious Muzio in the delightful song 'Colombetta'.

Heddle Nash sings Opera Arias and Songs. (Pearl GEMM CD 9319)

Nash was Britain's leading lyric tenor between the wars. He possessed a voice of rare beauty that always touched his hearers, and he always sang with a minstrel-like fervour as the examples of his art here indicate. He was a notable Don Ottavio in *Don Giovanni* and Duke of Mantua in *Rigoletto*, both well represented here. More fine examples of his art, including the whole of Act 4 of *La Bohème* and extracts from *Faust*, both conducted by Beecham, can be heard on *Heddle Nash – Vol 2* (GEMM CD 9473). He was also a notable Ferrando in Glyndebourne's first set of Mozart's *Così fan tutte* on EMI (qv).

Julius Patzak – Opera and Operetta Recital. (Pearl GEMM CD 9383)

After Tauber (qv), Patzak was the leading Austro-German tenor of the inter-war period. His peculiarly plangent voice and his inborn artistry graced everything he sang from Bach to operetta and Viennese popular songs. This disc has many of the best of his operatic offerings, ranging from Donizetti to Johann Strauss. All the interpretations are poised and thoughtful – but, beware, the Offenbach items are transferred up a tone or so.

Pavarotti Sings Verdi. (Sony CD 377228)

This is an unusual disc, including many rarely heard arias by Verdi, either from seldom-played works or discarded items. Most of Pavarotti's discs have been made for Decca, which have been assembled in all sorts of collections, details of which can be found in the GRAMOPHONE Classical Catalogue.

Ezio Pinza – Opera Recital. (Pearl GEMM CD 9306)

Pinza was leading bass at La Scala in the 1920s before moving to the Metropolitan where he remained until after the Second World War, when he took up a new career in musicals, most notably *South Pacific*. He had a bass voice of beauty, power and cutting edge, and his performances – particularly of Verdi – became the yardstick by which others have since been judged. His authority is self-evident here in discs made during the 1920s and '30s, ranging from Mozart through Bellini and Donizetti to Verdi where he was at his greatest.

Rosa Ponselle: Opera and Song Recital. (RCA GD 87810)

Having made an auspicious début in *La forza del destino* at the Metropolitan with Caruso (qv) in 1918, Ponselle went on to become one of the house's leading dramatic sopranos over the succeeding twenty years, most notable for her Leonoras, Norma, Gioconda and eventually Violetta. The voice was warm, slightly veiled in quality, and always employed thoughtfully. She was equally successful at Covent Garden in the seasons covering the years 1929 to 1931. Her art is well documented here.

Tito Schipa – Recital. (EMI CDH7 63200)

Schipa's long career lasted from 1911 to 1950. During that time his lyrical, plangent tenor was heard in a large opus of recordings. He was a much sought-after tenor in Europe and the United States for his Bellini, Donizetti, lighter Verdi and Puccini, and Massenet. (He was a notable Des Grieux and Werther.) He brought to them all a sovereign line, sense of style and feeling for the text. Like that of any great singer, his voice is immediately recognisable. Here he can be heard in arias from many of his most famous roles recorded by HMV at different stages of his career. In the middle of it he was contracted to Victor and further recommendable examples of his art are to be found on RCA GD 87965, few of which overlap with the EMI issue. (See also Donizetti: *Don Pasquale*.)

Riccardo Stracciari. (Preiser 89003)

Stracciari had one of the most compelling baritone voices and presences of the century. Renowned particularly for his Rossini Figaro and for his Rigoletto, he ranged over a wide repertory, as can be heard on this well-engineered reissue, a joy for anyone interested in great singing.

Conchita Supervia – Rossini and Bizet Arias. (EMI CDH7 63499-2)

Supervia, the Spanish mezzo, was one of the most engaging singers ever to grace a stage, and her ebullient presence was well caught on her records. The discs assembled here catch her prized Rossini heroines and her defiant, sexy Carmen to the life. They are a thing of joy for all time.

The Art of the Prima Donna. Joan Sutherland, Ch and O of the Royal Opera House, Covent Garden/Francesco Molinari-Pradelli. (Decca 425 493-2)

This legendary set, recorded (1960) in Sutherland's first flush of success, remains a landmark in twentieth-century singing. It includes excerpts from works by Arne, Handel, Mozart, Rossini, Bellini, Verdi, Delibes, Gounod, Meyerbeer, and Thomas. There are well-known showpieces which demonstrate the agility of the diva at this stage in her career, but we are also shown her gift for pathos in Bellini's 'Casta diva' (from *Norma*) and Desdemona's Willow Song from Verdi's *Otello*. Each item is related to a prima donna particularly associated with the music in hand. Sutherland's tone was then at its freshest and her style had not yet accumulated the tendency to be droopy that was soon to afflict her singing.

The Age of Belcanto. Arias and duets by Piccinni, Bononcini, Shield, Mozart, Boïeldieu, Rossini, Weber, Bellini, Graun. Joan Sutherland (with Marilyn Horne, Richard Conrad), various orchs/Richard Bonynge. (Decca 421 881-2)

A recording made shortly after the previous entry, once again showing Sutherland in corruscating form in material that was perfectly suited to her voice. Each item is once again devoted to the memory of a noted prima donna. Horne also contributes splendidly.

Richard Tauber – Opera Arias and Duets (with Elisabeth Rethberg and Lotte Lehmann). (EMI CDH7 64029-2)

Tauber was one of the most popular tenors of the century. His long career stretched from 1914 to 1947, during which his sappy, vibrant voice hardly deteriorated in character. At first a member of various German opera companies and then leading tenor at the Vienna State Opera, in the latter part of his career he became famed all over Europe in the operettas of Lehár. This disc fairly represents the operatic side of his art from his eloquent, stylish Mozart through to his Puccini, Offenbach and Tchaikovsky. Everything is given in the tenor's native German, in which Tauber sings with total freedom and an urge to communicate. Any sensitive listener will capitulate to his charm. Pearl has reissued other discs by Tauber.

Renata Tebaldi – the Early Recordings. Verdi: *Aida*, Act 3 (complete), arias by Verdi, Gounod, Puccini. (Decca 425 989-2)

Tebaldi was Callas's coeval. They were rivals for the attentions of the world's opera lovers in the early post-war decades, but in truth they were very different artists. Tebaldi possessed the more certain voice and the more orthodox manner, but little of Callas's ability to illumine a role from within. This disc restores to circulation Tebaldi's earliest and possibly her best recordings when her *spinto* soprano was at its freshest. It preserves some of the most natural and beautiful Verdi and Puccini singing of the century.

La Tebaldi. Arias by Rossini, Verdi, Puccini, Cilea, Boito, Giordamo, Catalani, Mascagni and Refice. (Decca 430 481-2) (two discs)

This collection derives from complete sets and recitals made by the diva between 1955 and 1968. It is a fair souvenir of her straightforward, heartfelt art.

Lawrence Tibbett sings Opera Arias. (RCA GD 87808)

Tibbett owned one of the roundest, most secure baritones of the century. He was in his prime between 1925 and 1940 when he was leading baritone at the Metropolitan taking most of the principal roles in the works of Verdi and Puccini. This is a welcome collection of arias including Figaro's Largo al factotum, the Prologue to *Pagliacci*, Renato's 'Eri tu' (*Un ballo in maschera*), Valentin's aria from *Faust* and Wolfram's aria from *Tannhäuser*. Few have received better sung performances than those Tibbett provides.

Dame Eva Turner sings Opera Arias and Songs. (EMI CDH7 69791)

Turner was the great English dramatic soprano of the inter-war years, who survived into the late 1980s, when – in her own nineties – she recorded a touching introduction to this reissue of her records. These include her legendary account of Turandot's steely solo, a version still to be surpassed for security and power. Turandot was Turner's most famous role – but she was also a notable Aida, Gioconda and Butterfly as this disc confirms. The reissue also includes a previously unissued account of Elisabeth's Greeting from *Tannhäuser*, put together by modern technical wizardy and loving care from a broken 78 of a test disc: it shows Turner at her best. Some lovely performances of songs complete this welcome reissue.

Ljuba Welitsch: Opera Recital (EMI CDH7 61007-2)

Welitsch, one of the most exciting sopranos of the early postwar era, crossed the operatic firmament like a meteor and was all too soon extinguished. Salome was her most compelling role, and her war-time account of the opera's final scene, included here, has never been surpassed. Here, too are souvenirs of her appreciable Tatyana, Aïda and Tosca, among others. Her tone, clear, strong, glinting is memorable.

Fritz Wunderlich – Great German Tenor. (EMI CZS7 62993-2)

Wunderlich was the most notable German tenor of the 1950s and early '60s, who died untimely at the age of 36, following an accident in 1966. He left a vast number of recordings to remind us of the beauty and style of his singing. This selection includes examples of his refined, warm Mozart and his charm in operetta. It also has him in several French and Italian roles, usually singing in his native German. In all he maintains his faultless voice production, even if the idiom isn't always wholly comprehensible.

INDEX